TALKS WITH TOLSTOY

WITH TOLSTOY

BY

A. B. GOLDENWEIZER

Goldenveizer, A. B.

TRANSLATED BY

S. S. KOTELIANSKY AND VIRGINIA WOOLF

INTRODUCTION BY

HENRY LE ROY FINCH

HORIZON PRESS
NEW YORK

INTRODUCTION

It was Dostoevsky who, speaking of *Anna Karenina,* wrote that "everything, even the smallest detail, shows the beautiful unity of the temperament from which it flows." This expression, by Tolstoy's undoubted literary peer, describes with great accuracy what remains the most striking fact about Tolstoy—his quality of being "all-of-a-piece," his unity and wholeness. All the contradictions and conflicts of his life—between his physical nature and his imperious will, between the demands of his teaching and those of his wife and family, between the requirements of the artist and of the moralist—none of these ever impaired this fundamental wholeness. The struggles with himself, with his wife and children and with his age never signified any basic brokenness, but rather always new efforts toward self-development.

This is bound to seem surprising to us because Tolstoy was a rebel, and we are accustomed, for the most part, to rebellion which arises from, and feeds upon, alienation. Tolstoy's rebellion—and no one went further in rebellion than he—does not fit this pattern because it harbored no resentment against grievances, no inner inadequacy or negativity, no irreparable barrier between himself and the world. It sprang rather from the attempt to translate the wholeness that he knew into life. Perhaps never has a writer, an artist, or a prophet been less alienated or more at home in the world than Tolstoy. Unlike Dostoevsky, who seemed marked from birth as an outcast (he lived his earliest years in a big city hospital surrounded by misery and suffering) and believed that all human things have their roots in other worlds, Tolstoy knew of no other world than this one. But the world that he was at home in was not the modern world with its violence, greed and power-lust, but a more primeval, a more natural world, the world before the Fall. If, as he grew older, he rejected many youthful joys, it was because they were not "natural" enough, or "natural" only in a limited, selfish and personal sense. "Natural" for him never meant "animal"; it meant, as it did for the Stoics, "naturally human." And what was "naturally human" was not to follow animal impulses but to follow uncorrupted reason and conscience.

There was in Tolstoy, as also in Dostoevsky in a different way, something like a *passion for goodness*. With his alarming candor he wrote as a young man:

"I love goodness and have formed the habit of loving it," but then added: "But there is something I love even more than goodness—fame."[1] In some ways it was fame which was almost his undoing; for in middle life when he had achieved it, he had to find in his own interpretation of Christianity a still more universal meaning for goodness in order that life might continue to have meaning; and in old age it made his life a gold-fish bowl and his relations with his family all but impossible. Goodness continued to mean a natural human nobility, but now beyond all separate being and beyond all limits of self-interest and self-gratification. As a young man he had prayed:

> Help me, not for the satisfaction of my insignificant aims, but for the eternal great and unseen aim of my existence of which I am conscious. (Diary of 1855.)

And as an old man he wrote:

> A mistake (sin) is the use of reason, given me to recognize my essence in the love of everything which exists, in acquiring the good for my separate being. (Diary of 1896.)

[1]Diary of 1853. Unless otherwise specified, references to Tolstoy's diaries are to the following volumes: *The Private Diary of Leo Tolstoy 1853-1857*, translated by A. Maude (London, 1927); *The Journal of Leo Tolstoy 1895-1899*, translated by Rose Strunsky (New York, 1917); and *The Final Struggle— Being Countess Tolstoy's Diary for 1910 with Extracts from Leo Tolstoy's Diary for the Same Period*, translated by A. Maude (London, 1936).

There is a single ever-present theme running through Tolstoy's life like a bass-motif, his conviction that, important as art is, *there is a human task which exceeds the task of art.* It is that of moral self-perfecting, *the task of becoming a man.* Tolstoy never ceased to put this first—the obligation of a human being to work on himself, to struggle to perfect himself. He always regarded this as the principal aim of life, without which life could not be lived. Three quotations from different periods of his life illustrate this conviction. At the end of an early book, the autobiographical *Boyhood,* the narrator, speaking of a youthful friend, says:

> I unconsciously adopted his view, the gist of which consisted in an enthusiastic adoration of the ideal of virtue, and in a belief that man is intended constantly to perfect himself.

Twenty-five years later *Anna Karenina* closes with these words, spoken by Levin:

> My life now, my whole life, apart from anything that can happen to me, every minute of it is no more meaningless, but it has the positive meaning of goodness which I have the power to put into it.

And, finally, another twenty-five years later when he was seventy-seven, it is all summed up in his diary:

> All that is good in life, all that is right, every real action is accomplished by effort. Renounce effort and you let yourself drift with the current, you do not live. Neverthe-

less, the Church teaches that all effort is a sin of pride—confidence in one's own powers; and lay organization repeats that personal effort is vain, and that organization and environment do everything. What a mistake! Personal effort, no matter how small, is the essential thing. To conquer laziness, gluttony, envy, anger and depression—this is the most important thing in the world; it is the testimony of the divine in life, it is Karma, the development of the self.[2]

This fundamental theme of the human obligation to strive for moral perfection pervades the present book through Goldenweizer's recollections of Tolstoy. As he was leaving Yasnaya after one of his first visits, Goldenweizer reports Tolstoy as saying to him:

I have been meaning all this time to tell you, and now as you are going I shall tell you: however great a gift for music you may have, and however much time and power you may spend on it, do remember that, above all, the most important of all is to be a man. It is always necessary to remember that art is not everything. (p. 14.)

Later Tolstoy speaks to him of "the enormously important question of how to live one's life in the best and most moral way" (p. 24), and at another point, refusing to separate writer and man, says: "The whole business of the writer is to perfect himself" (p. 139).

[2]Diaries of 1895-99, quoted by Derrick Leon in *Tolstoy—His Life and Work* (London, 1944), p. 294, from the French translation by N. Rostowa and M. Jean-Debrit (Paris, 1910). This passage does not appear in the English translation by Rose Strunsky.

9

From the age of fifteen, when Tolstoy began to draw up rules for himself "according to the manner of Franklin," he never gave up his conviction that a man could improve himself if he tried. Year after year his diaries record his attempts to overcome his faults, itemizing day-by-day what he has done wrong and trying especially "to cure myself of my three main vices—irritability, lack of character and idleness." (This can be compared with the list of the three main human vices given to Goldenweizer forty years later: "(1) anger, malevolence; (2) vanity; and (3) lust in the widest sense of the word" [p. 53].) At one point in 1855, when he was approaching thirty, he writes:

> It is ridiculous that, having started writing rules at fifteen, when nearly thirty, I am still writing them, without having trusted or followed any of them, and yet I still believe in them and want them. (Diary of 1855.)

At sixty-eight, remembering a childhood misdeed, he says touchingly:

> One must suffer humiliation and be good. I can do it. (Diary of 1893.)

And two months before his death:

> As far as moral perfection is concerned I feel like a youngster, a schoolboy, and not a very assiduous schoolboy yet. (Diary of 1910.)

It is the calm and settled conviction that human beings *can* improve themselves and that moral con-

siderations always come first and *must* come first
which, perhaps more than anything else, makes Tolstoy so compelling and attractive. Smaller-minded
traffickers in power, who in every age make up the
political spectrum, will scarcely understand his remark to Goldenweizer that "I always consider that
moral motives are effective and decisive historically"
(p. 38). Nor will conventional revolutionaries understand any better his remark about them that "Their
chief mistake is the superstition that one can arrange
human life" (p. 160). In Tolstoy's view it is not
within our power to "arrange" life ahead of time (and
one should not attempt to do so [p. 173]), since
what happens, even in an individual life, is most often
the result of innumerable unknown factors and many
human wills over which no single person has any
control. What *is* within our power is our own behavior
and the attitude which we take toward events, and it
is this which can be decisive, since it directly affects
other people. This is why Tolstoy says: "The only true
way for a man to improve human life is by the way
of moral perfection in his personal life" (p. 74).[3]

[3] In a famous article published in 1908, Lenin praised Tolstoy's condemnation of capitalism in Russia but castigated him
and the Tolstoyans for abstaining from politics and for putting
personal morality first. Since the Soviet experience with Stalin,
it is doubtful that even orthodox Marxists can any longer so
quickly dismiss the question of personal morality.

Something like a Protestant conscience (Tolstoy's affinity to Kant, whom he praises so highly to Goldenweizer, should not be underestimated) stands at the center of Tolstoy's religious experience. Both faith and religion are defined in moral terms. Faith, for example, is described in one place as "man's consciousness that his position in the world obliges him to do certain things" and religion as "composed of simple, apparent, clear, indubitable moral truths, which are separated from the chaos of false and deceptive judgments." He tells us that

> Religion is the consciousness of those truths which are universally accessible to all men, in all their situations, at all times, and are as indubitable as that two times two are four.[4]

In this understanding of religion there is no room for the mysterious, the fantastic, the super-real, which comprise the very essence of religion for Dostoevsky. The other-worldliness of Dostoevsky (dating from his early "vision at the Neva" and running through all his work), the belief that what happens in this world is the manifestation of unseen forces in other worlds, has no reality for Tolstoy. The world of the senses, of innocence and delight, could not be a phantasmagoria for an imagination of such concreteness! It is misleading to follow critical fashion and, with-

[4] *Thoughts and Aphorisms*, "Religion," included in the *Complete Works of Tolstoy* (London, 1905), Vol. XIX, p. 78.

out further ado, divide Tolstoy's career into two parts, assigning the first part to the artist and the second part, after his "conversion," to the moralist. From the beginning art as such was never enough for Tolstoy. The dominating impulse of his writing was *always* a moral one. It is the young Tolstoy at the beginning of his career who said:

> I am astonished that we should have lost the conception of the one aim of literature—morality—to such a degree that if you were to speak nowadays of the necessity for morality in literature, no one would understand you.[5]

It is true, of course, that in the second half of his life, when his ideas about art had developed fully, Tolstoy spoke disapprovingly of his earlier writings. They were, he said, lacking in universality because they dealt with, and were addressed to, only a particular class of society. (Indeed, the very question of the double meaning of the word "society" was at stake, for how long could a small group of people continue to lay claim to being "society"?) Speaking to Goldenweizer about his compilation of readings for each day of the month—the "Circle of Reading"—he says:

> At the beginning of each day I put the ideas that can be understood by children and simple people. This is very difficult. I am doing it now when I am an old man, but I

[5]Leon, *op cit.*, p. 43, quoting from the Diary of 1847-52, in the French translation. This passage does not appear in the English translation by Rose Strunsky.

ought to have begun my career as a writer by doing it. I ought to have written so that it could have been understood by every one. This is true, too, of your art. And, generally speaking, of all the arts. (p. 167.)

The demand on art that he had always recognized—that it should contribute to the strength and beauty of life—had been broadened to the demand that art should be for everyone, and this was coupled with the realization that the greatest strength and beauty lay with the simplest people—the peasants.

We do not get an accurate picture, however, if we say merely that Tolstoy subordinated art to morality or imposed moral requirements on art. The relationship between art and morality was for him far more intimate than this; there is even a sense in which his conception of morality was itself rooted in his conception of art. The two were inseparable because he always understood art as having to do with *objective truth* and not merely with private invention. It was the objective eye of the artist which rose above all purely personal passions to report the world as it was. Art, Tolstoy believed, should be impersonal and impartial, the artist using his whole being as an instrument of perception to mirror the world faithfully.

This artistic credo was formulated very early and is expressed in the Diary of 1851:

Imagination is the mirror of nature; a mirror which we carry within ourselves, and in which nature is por-

14

trayed. The finest imagination is the clearest and truest
mirror—that mirror which we call genius! Genius does
not create; it reflects.[6]

(In this there is a reminder of a similar, well-known
remark made by Goethe:

> I permit objects to make their impression upon me
> quietly. I observe the effect and endeavor to reproduce
> it faithfully and without vitiation. That is the whole
> secret of what men are pleased to call genius.)

At the end of the early story, *Sevastopol in May,* there
is another testimony to truthfulness as the aim of art:

> The hero of my tale, whom I love with all the strength
> of my soul, whom I have tried to set forth in all his
> beauty, and who has always been, is, and always will be
> most beautiful is—the truth.

For Tolstoy there remained no higher court of
appeal in art than the truth.[7] And the truth meant

[6]Leon, *op. cit.,* p. 41.

[7]In his lectures delivered at the Lowell Institute in Boston in
Boston in 1901 and published under the title of *Ideals and Re-
alities in Russian Literature* (New York, 1916), Peter Kropotkin said of Tolstoy: "Notwithstanding Tolstoy's distrust of science, I must say that I always feel in reading his works that he
is possessed of the most *scientific* insight I know of among
artists. He may be wrong in his conclusions, but never is he
wrong in his statement of data" (p. 117). As an anarchist,
Kropotkin shared many views with Tolstoy but did not put the
same emphasis on non-violence. (cf. Paul Eltzbacher, *Anarchism* (New York, 1960), a book which Tolstoy praised to
Goldenweizer [p. 47] when it was first published in German
in 1900.)

freedom from personal distortions, subjective intrusions and special pleadings. The universality and impersonality of art are fully implicit in such a view, and it is not difficult to see the morality of his later years as a further development of this artistic credo. There is not so great a gap between art as the impersonal portrayal of what exists and love as the impersonal acceptance of what exists. In the famous passage from *War and Peace,* as Prince Andrey lies dying he reflects:

> And I know this blissful feeling now too. To love one's neighbors, to love one's enemies. To love everything— to love God in all his manifestations. Someone dear to one can be loved with human love, but an enemy can only be loved with divine love. . . . Loving with human love one may pass from love to hatred; but divine love cannot change. Nothing, not even death, nothing can shatter it. It is the very nature of the soul.

The moral universality reached here in Christian terms is twin to the artistic universality implicit in the objective impartiality of art as Tolstoy conceived it.

As a literary artist Tolstoy practiced what might be called *whole-seeing,* or seeing with the fullness of response of a child. As Goldenweizer says, he always gives us a *clear, definite picture* (p. 15, italics added), and this is possible because there is a freshness and spontaneity in the ever-changing, but always wholehearted, balance of observation, feeling and emotion.

Tolstoy's own happy childhood is always in the background, furnishing the model for what he meant by love and faith, and for the naturalness and simplicity of the life to which he aspired.

> Happy, happy childhood, that blissful time never to be recalled! How can I help loving it and cherishing its bright memories? Those memories refresh and elevate my soul, they are a source of never-ending joy to me. . . . Will that freshness, that light-heartedness, that necessity for love, that strength of faith which one possessed in childhood, ever return? (*Childhood,* Chapter XV.)

In Tolstoy's sense it is the child who is capable of the truth, without giving it a second thought. But at the same time, the child's world revolves around itself, and the unthinking cruelty of the self-centered is part of its warp and woof. In the Diary of 1898 he refers to this:

> Children are selfish without lies. All of life teaches the aimlessness, the ruination of selfishness. And therefore old people attain unselfishness without lies. These are the two extreme limits.

He might have added that in between is the bulk of life—*selfishness with lies.*

The wholeness of the child, however, contains the seed of its own destruction because it is not yet conscious, and the child has not yet faced the contradiction of its own limitation: that what it demands others demand for themselves too and that as an individual

17

it is doomed in one way or another to death and destruction. Slowly, as reason awakens, the emerging man begins to understand this contradiction as an inescapable reality. And now the realization may begin to dawn that there are two natures in us—the animal, doomed to destruction, and the spiritual or rational, which sees and understands and which cannot be destroyed.

What follows then is expressed in Tolstoy's most important philosophical work—*On Life,* written in 1887. Here at last he reaches the conclusion that

> Man's true life begins only when the sacrifice of his animal personality commences. And this sacrifice begins when his reasonable consciousness awakens.

In Tolstoy's view human beings have no choice but to liberate the "I" of the spirit from the animal personality, because, from the time that reason has been awakened and has shown the contradiction of the merely personal life, happiness becomes possible only in the terms laid down by that reason. As he says to Goldenweizer: ". . . happiness is only possible when the struggle for personal happiness is renounced" (p. 46). Reason is misapplied when it takes the separate physical existence of the individual as true life, not realizing that it is just *this reason itself* which is our real life beyond space and time.

Tolstoy's message here is more Stoic and Buddhistic than it is specifically Christian. In linking what is per-

sonal with physical separateness and what is impersonal with the rational and the spiritual, he creates a
rationalistic version of Christianity at the expense of
its personalistic character. In the Judeo-Christian tra-
dition it is *not* particularity, finiteness or separateness
which separates us from God, but *only* the illusory
divinity of the ego. Tolstoy's rationalism leads him to
an abstract universalism which surrenders the paradoxical character of Christianity—that paradoxical relation of the finite and the infinite, the temporal and
the eternal, which inspires the Christian. But, whatever else he was prepared to sacrifice, Tolstoy was not
prepared to sacrifice his intellect.

Tolstoy's asceticism, like Nietzsche's "hardness," or
the Stoic *apatheia* (passionlessness), or the discipline
of traditional Hinduism and Buddhism, has an aristo-
cratic character in the sense that it rests on the premise
that nothing is achieved except at the price of sacrifice
and work. Such Christian doctrines as gratuitous
grace, vicarious atonement, and the undeserved love
of God—signs of the incomprehensible which violate
all sense of natural justice—could never be acceptable
to a man who began his re-translation of the New
Testament by rendering the opening verse of the
Fourth Gospel, "In the beginning was the Word," as
"The comprehension of life became the beginning
of all."[8]

[8]*The Four Gospels Harmonized and Translated* (Boston,
1904), Vol. I, p. 24.

Somewhere near this point is the center of the vast theological dialogue between Tolstoy and Dostoevsky which continues today and will continue far into the future with ever greater intensity and increasingly momentous consequences. On the one side is the great prophet of the normal, remembering the happiness of childhood and dreaming of "the religion of Christ, purged of dogmas and mysticism . . . giving bliss on earth," and on the other the equally great prophet of the abnormal, haunted all his life by the unjustified suffering of children and sure that, in the words of the "underground man," "man will never give up true suffering, that is to say destruction and chaos."

The sacredness of suffering and evil—this is the awesome theme of Dostoevsky. "On our earth we can only love with suffering and through suffering . . . in suffering alone there is meaning," says the "ridiculous man." Man loves suffering and clings to it because it is the proof of his freedom. And without evil and suffering there would be no limit to human delusions, no bounds to our arrogance. We might then, being no longer able to distinguish between sham and reality, fall under the final delusion that this earth, this "purgatory of human spirits," as Dostoevsky called it, was in fact, as arranged by reason, already paradise.

A vast distance separates the two—the one who could not bring himself to doubt that "two plus two equals four" and the other who could not bring himself to accept it. When Tolstoy was ill in the Crimea in 1901 and not expected to live, he refused to see a priest sent by the Hold Synod, which had long before excommunicated him, saying to his son:

> How is it, Sergey, that these gentlemen do not understand that even in the face of death two and two still make four?[9]

Years before, Dostoevsky's "underground man" had railed:

> What have I to do with the laws of nature or with arithmetic when all the time those laws and the formula that twice two makes four do not meet with my acceptance?[10]

For, he says, "two times two is four" is the "beginning of death" because it limits our freedom and nothing must limit our freedom.

> Twice two is four, after all, is a truly insufferable thing. Twice two is four, why this, in my opinion is simply an effrontery, sir. Twice two is four looks like a fop, stands across your road, arms akimbo and spits. I am agreed that twice two is four is an excellent thing, but if we are to give everything its due, then twice two is five is also sometimes a very charming little thing.

[9]This story is told in a footnote appended by Aylmer Maude in *The Final Struggle*, p. 364.

[10]This and the following quotations from Dostoevsky are from *Notes from the Underground*. For the importance of this document, see Robert Louis Jackson, *Dostoevsky's Underground Man in Russian Literature* ('S-Gravenhage, 1958).

If the mystery of suffering and evil is a scandal to human reason, then, says Dostoevsky, so much the worse for human reason. Again the "underground man":

> Suffering . . . this is the sole cause of consciousness . . . Consciousness . . . is infinitely superior to twice two is four.

More important than any reason is man's right, in the name of his freedom and of his suffering, to reject even the truths of arithmetic.

For Dostoevsky evil may be done in full knowledge that it is evil (and he echoes St. Augustine's horrified cry: "I was in love with the evil just because it was evil!"), and the most elevated nobility and utter depravity may exist side by side in the same soul. Further (and this is what he learned in the "house of the dead" in Siberia), evil is a spiritual force (perhaps even of superhuman dimensions) and not merely an inadvertence or a surrender to physical impulses. What, from Dostoevsky's point of view, Tolstoy failed to see is that evil has a reality of its own, may even represent a triumph over the physical, and may even be, in its own way, completely "rational." Perhaps Tolstoy had never seen such cases; but Dostoevsky had seen them—in Siberia.

What is Tolstoy's answer to this? Part of it was given to Gorky when he said about Dostoevsky:

He ought to have made himself acquainted with the teaching of Confucius or the Buddhists; that would have calmed him down. That is the chief thing which everyone should know. He was a man of rebellious flesh when angry, bumps would suddenly rise on his bald head, and his ears would move. He felt a great deal, but he thought poorly. . . . It is all painful and useless, because all those Idiots, Adolescents, Raskolnikovs, and the rest of them, they are not real; it is all much simpler, more understandable.[11]

What Tolstoy thought about evil emerges in a remark in the Diary of 1853:

The description of a struggle between good and evil in a man who is committing, or has just committed, an evil action, always seems to me unnatural. Evil is done easily and unconsciously, and only much later does the man become horrified and amazed at what he has done.

In the Diary of 1897 he notes:

It is remarkable how many people see some insoluble problem in evil. I have never seen any problem in it. For me it is now altogether clear that that which we call evil is that good the action of which we don't yet see.

Is evil a separate reality, or is it merely an absence of good or a good not yet seen? St. Augustine and the church fathers wrestled with this, trying to steer a path between the twin menaces of Manichean dualism

[11]Maxim Gorky, *Reminiscences of Tolstoy, Checkov and Andreev* (London, 1948), p. 65.

23

on the one side and neo-Platonic pantheism on the other.

In Dostoevsky rebellion goes to the bottom of his soul, so deep that he must "put the darkness into God" in the name of freedom and of all the hurt and suffering of the world, which no art or nature or reason or morality can justify or remove. The hurt is so deep that even Christ himself, whom (as he wrote his brother from prison) he loved even more than truth, no longer suffices to wipe it out. Nothing can justify the never-ending stream of human suffering, and if man chooses to live forever in rebellion, then God Himself must remain powerless before this accumulated agony.

What has Tolstoy to put up against this? His books tell us: the happiness and joy of life, the clear reconciling light of day, the observing eye which rises above all the abysses and agonies of the spirit. What we cannot accept, life accepts for us, and even those who, having nothing else, cling to their misery and pain may find that life itself still struggles to release them. Dostoevsky knew this because at the end of his last book he, too, celebrated the "sticky green leaves" and the laughter of the children. And Tolstoy knew what must be done with suffering. "Suffering," he said, "is not an evil which you must be rid of, but the work of your life which you must accept."[12]

[12]Leon, *op cit.,* p. 294.

24

In the end the two giants join hands—the one, Dostoevsky, who believed that *we are lived by ideas* and that ideas are titanic extra-mundane forces, "inert, mighty and of all-engulfing power," and the other, Tolstoy, who told us that

Thoughts are the beginning of everything and *thoughts can be directed.* And therefore the principal task of perfection is to work on thoughts. (Diary of 1899, italics added.)

The two great thaumaturgists—the one conjuring up spirits from the deep and the other looking straight through everything with an eye "like a thousand eyes" —shared more than they knew.By different roads both were on the way to the great goal of *kenosis,* or self-emptying, imitating the Russian Christ. "No one has ever stooped half low enough to find the truth," said an ancient sage. Both these men went down into humiliation to find humility and to find their oneness with others. As he finished the *Brothers Karamazov* and turned again to the *Diary of a Writer,* Dostoevsky wrote to a friend:

I've often and repeatedly now prayed on my knees to God, that he give me a pure heart, a word that is pure, sinless, not irritable, not envious.[13]

And in the whole of literature there is perhaps nothing

[13]Quoted in Konstantin Mochulsky, *Dostoevsky—His Life and Work* (Princeton, 1967), p. 644.

more touching than Tolstoy's description of himself toward the end of his life:

> I am only a weak man of evil habits, who desires to serve the God of Truth, but continually goes astray.[14]

HENRY LEROY FINCH
Sarah Lawrence College
June, 1969

[14] From a letter quoted by Aylmer Maude in *The Life of Tolstoy: Later Years* (London, 1910), p. 436.

PUBLISHER'S NOTE

The spelling of Tolstoy on the title-page and in Henry Le Roy Finch's introduction to this edition accords with contemporary usage, but it has been kept intact in the following pages which are printed in facsimile reproduction of the original edition.

TRANSLATORS' NOTE

In the following pages we have made a selection from vol. i. of the diary of the well-known Russian musician, A. B. Goldenveizer, which was published at the end of 1922 in Moscow under the title *Vblizi Tolstovo* (literally *Near Tolstoi*).

INTRODUCTORY NOTE

In publishing the diary devoted to my friend-
ship of nearly fifteen years with Leo Nikolaevich
Tolstoi, I think it best to state first what my aim
was in making notes, and the method I pursued
in doing so.

I put down chiefly Tolstoi's words, and to
some extent the events of his private life, making
no attempt to select what would be interesting
from some special point of view, but adopting
no method and attempting to supply no connection between one entry and another.

My diary, therefore, is in no sense "literature."
Its aim is to be a document.

Unfortunately, I did not always make notes
and was far from writing down everything.
After 1908 my records were fuller; in 1909–
1910, the last year of Tolstoi's life, my reports
were voluminous; but it was only in 1910 that
my records were as complete as they could

possibly be. This is the cause of a great disproportion between the parts. The first volume of my diary contains the long period from January 1896 to January 1st, 1910, the second volume records and materials for the year 1910 only, yet vol. ii. is considerably larger than vol. i.

My notes from 1896 to 1904 are now published for the first time. The notes from 1904 to 1908 were published in *Russ. Prop.* vol. ii., and the notes from the end of 1908 to January 1st, 1910, appeared in *Tolstoi: Pamyatniki Zhizni i Tvorchestva.* The parts of the diary which have been previously published are here published in a considerably enlarged form.

A. GOLDENWEIZER.

1896

...irst visit to the house of Leo Nikolaevich
... on January 20th, 1896. I was not then
...nty-one years old. I was almost a boy. I
...s taken to the Tolstois' by a well-known
...loscow lady singer who used to visit the
Tolstois. She took me there in my capacity as
pianist, of course. If one is so unlucky as to
play some instrument, or to sing or recite, one
has a constant impediment in one's relations
with people. People do not take to one, are
not interested in one as in a person : one is asked
to play something, to sing, to recite. . . .
Hence one feels so embarrassed, so awkward, in
other people's society.

I felt awkward then, and painfully shy. I
was introduced. I went into the drawing-room,
where, fortunately, two or three people I knew
were sitting. I did not yet see Tolstoi. Shortly
afterwards he came in, dressed in a blouse, with
his hands in his belt. He greeted us all. I do

not remember whether he spoke to me th
Then I played, and played badly. Of cour
out of politeness I was thanked and comp
mented, which made me inexpressibly ashame
And then, when I stood in the middle of th
large room, at a loss, not knowing what to do
with myself, not daring to raise my eyes, Leo
Nikolaevich came up to me, and, speaking with
a simplicity which was his alone, began to talk
to me.

Among other things, talking of the piece I
had played, he asked me :

" Which composer do you like best ? "

" Beethoven," I replied.

Tolstoi looked straight into my eyes and
said quietly as if doubting me :

" Is that so ? "

It seemed as if I were repeating what every
one says ; but I spoke the truth.

Leo Nikolaevich observed that he loved
Chopin beyond almost all other composers.

He said to me :

" In every art—this I know from my own
experience too—there are two extremes which
it is difficult to avoid : emptiness and virtuosity.
For instance, Mozart, whom I love so much, is
at times empty, but after that he soars to an
extraordinary height. Schumann's defect is virtu-

osity. Of these two faults virtuosity is the worse, if only for this reason, that it is harder to get rid of it. Chopin's greatness consists in the fact that, however simple he may be, he is never empty, and in his most complicated works he is never a mere virtuoso."

I left the Tolstois' house with a vague feeling of happiness that I had seen Tolstoi and spoken to him, and also with a bitter sense of my own unworthiness.

One evening as I approached the Tolstois' house in Khamovniki I met Leo Nikolaevich, who was going for a walk. He asked me to come with him. We walked in the Prechistenka. The street was deserted and quiet. The few passers-by whom we met at intervals nearly all bowed to Leo Nikolaevich. By degrees Leo Nikolaevich brought me to talk about myself. At that time I was carried away by the philosophy of pessimism; I raved about Schopenhauer. Probably everything I said to Leo Nikolaevich was naïve and silly, but Leo Nikolaevich listened to me attentively and spoke to me seriously without making me feel my naïveté.

In passing, Leo Nikolaevich said to me :

" The most complete and profound philosophy is to be found in the Gospels."

I remember that at that time it seemed to me

strange. I was used to thinking the Gospels a book of moral teaching ; and I did not understand that all the wisdom of the most profound philosophy was contained in its simplicity and lucidity.

Once I met Leo Nikolaevich in the street. He again asked me to walk with him. We were somewhere near the Novinsky Boulevard, and Leo Nikolaevich suggested we should take the tram. We sat down and took our tickets.

Leo Nikolaevich asked me :

" Can you make a Japanese cockerel ? "

" No."

" Look."

Tolstoi took his ticket and very skilfully made it into a rather elaborate cockerel, which, when you pulled its tail, fluttered its wings.

An inspector entered the car and began checking the tickets. L. N., with a smile, held out the cockerel to him and pulled its tail. The cockerel fluttered its wings. But the inspector, with the stern expression of a business man who has no time for trifling, took the cockerel, unfolded it, looked at the number, and tore it up.

L. N. looked at me and said :

" Now our little cockerel is gone." . . .

I arrived at Yasnaya on July 6th after eleven o'clock at night.

I got up early in the morning and went to the river with L. N. to bathe. L. N. works every day from breakfast till lunch. He seemed to me to be in good spirits. In the morning at coffee he said :

" I feel as though I were nineteen or twenty."

Yasnaya then used to be crowded and gay. Nearly all the children were at home. All the young people played tennis and enjoyed themselves. Occasionally L. N. would also play tennis. In the evening all used to go out for long walks in the woods. L. N. always loved to find short cuts, and would take us all into wonderful places in the forests. It must be admitted that the 'short-cuts' nearly always made the walks longer.

Once L. N. and myself were left far behind the others. L. N. said : " Let us catch them up ! " And for half a mile or three-quarters I, twenty-one years old, and he, sixty-eight, ran neck and neck. On another occasion his physical vigour struck me even more. Mikhail Lvovich was doing a very difficult gymnastic exercise which he could not bring off. L. N. looked and looked, could not stand it any longer, and said : " Let me try," and to the surprise of all present he at once did the exercise better than his son.

When I was leaving Yasnaya and my carriage was waiting for me, L. N. took my arm, led me aside, and said :

" I have been meaning all this time to tell you, and now as you are going I shall tell you : however great a gift for music you may have, and however much time and power you may spend on it, do remember that, above all, the most important of all is to be a man. It is always necessary to remember that art is not everything. . . . In your relations with people it is necessary to try to give them as much as possible and to take from them as little as possible. Forgive me for saying this, but I did not want to say good-bye to you without having told you what I think."

Another of L. N.'s sayings at this time was : " The ego is the temporary thing that limits our immortal essence. Belief in personal immortality always seems to me a misunderstanding.

" Materialism is the most mystical of all doctrines : it makes a belief in some mythical matter, which creates everything out of itself, the foundation of everything. It is sillier than a belief in the Trinity ! "

1897

Moscow, January 6th. To-day I spent the evening at the Tolstois'. L. N. was talkative. The conversation was on various topics, beginning with the peasants and ending with the latest " decadent " movement in art.

L. N. read aloud certain passages of Maeterlinck's new play *Aglavaine et Sélysette.* His attitude to it is one of complete indifference.

L. N. reads aloud most wonderfully; very simply and at the same time with remarkable expression. Wonderful also is his capacity of telling in a few words the contents of a story. There is nothing superfluous, and a clear, definite picture is given.

April 22nd. At the Tolstois'.

Speaking of modern art, L. N. said :

" If an impressionist was asked to draw a hoop, he would draw a straight line —— ; a child would draw a circle like this ◯ " (L. N.

made the circle with his finger on the table). " And the child is more in the right, because he naïvely represents what he sees, and the impressionist represents what may be a hoop or a stick or anything you like ; in a word, he does not represent the characteristic properties of the thing, but only a symbol of it, a part, and that not always the most characteristic one.

" A really remarkable and powerful mind can look for a method of expressing his idea, and if the idea is strong he will find new methods of expressing it. But modern artists invent a technical method and then are on the look-out for an idea, which they arbitrarily squeeze into their method.

" The great mistake is that people have introduced into art the vague conception of ' beauty,' which obscures and confuses everything. . . . Art consists in this—when some one sees or feels something, and expresses it in such a form that he who listens, reads, or sees his work feels, sees, and hears the same thing in the same way as the artist. Therefore art can be of the highest quality, or indifferent, or, finally, simply hateful, but still it is art. The most immoral picture if it achieves its end is art, although it serves low ends.

" If I yawn, cry, or laugh, and infect another

person by the same thing, that is not art, for I produce the impression by the fact itself; but, if a beggar, for instance, seeing that his tears affected you and you gave him money, should on the following day pretend to cry and should arouse pity in you, then that is art."

August 2nd, 4 P.M. I have just had a long talk with L. N. on art. He was repeating the contents of his article on art which he is writing, and which he goes on working over and re-writing. In the course of it L. N. said :

"When art became the inheritance of a small circle of rich people, and left its main course, it entered the cul-de-sac in which we see it now.

"Art is the expression of feeling, and the higher it is the greater the public which it can draw to itself. Therefore the highest art must reflect those states of mind which are religious in the best sense of the word, as they are the most universal and typical of all human beings.

"The majority of so-called works of art consist in a more or less skilful combination of four elements : (1) borrowing—for instance, the working out of some legend in a poem, of a song in music, etc. Or unconscious borrowing—-that is, an imitation now of one thing, now of another, not intended by the author. (2) Embellishments : pretty metaphors which cover up insignificant ideas, flourishes in music, ornament in architecture, etc. (3) Effects : violent colours in painting, accumulated dissonances, sharp crescendos in music, and so on. Finally, (4) the interest—that is, the desire to surprise by the novelty of the method, by the new combination of colours, etc. Modern works of art are usually distinguished by these four qualities.

" The following are the chief obstacles which hinder even very remarkable men from creating true works of art : first, professionalism—that is, a man ceases to be a man, but becomes a poet, a painter, and does nothing but write books, compose music, or paint pictures ; wastes his gift on trifles and loses the power of judging his work critically. The second, also a very serious obstacle, is the school. You can't teach art, as you cannot teach a man to be a saint. True art is always original and new, and has no need of preconceived models. The third obstacle, finally, is criticism, which, as some one has justly said, is made up of fools' ideas about wise men.

" I know that my article will be received by most people as a series of paradoxes, but I am convinced that I am right."

L. N. is evidently much carried away by his work.

August 9th. This evening I am going to leave Yasnaya Polyana, where I have spent nearly a fortnight. The whole time passed wonderfully well. The days were spent more or less in this way : After breakfast every one goes to his work. L. N. takes his barley-coffee in a little kettle, and with the kettle in one hand and a few little pieces of bread in the other he goes to his room to work there, and does not come out till lunch.

A Note without a Date. In the summer of 1897 the famous Lombroso came to Yasnaya. I was not at Yasnaya at the time, but from what L. N. and others told me I can say that Lombroso, whose writings L. N. regarded without enthusiasm, had made no particular impression personally. I will give one example to show how superficially and inaccurately Lombroso related what he saw in Yasnaya. There was a round patch on one of L. N.'s boots, which came off, and L. N., while waiting to send the boot to be repaired, wore it with the hole in it. At that time Sophie Andreevna, I believe, took a snapshot of L. N., and the little hole on the boot was clearly seen in the photograph. I have that snapshot. Lombroso, in describing his visit to Yasnaya in the Press and in numerous interviews, said that L. N. pretended the 'simple life,' and, wanting to show that he wore torn boots, had made a round hole in one of them, evidently cut on purpose.

1899

May 11*th*. The conversation turned upon
Katkov.   L. N. expressed the opinion that
Katkov was not clever.   Sophie Andreevna
became annoyed and said :

" Any one who disagrees with us must be a
fool."

To which L. N. said :

" The mark of foolish people is : when you
say anything to them they never answer your
words, but keep on repeating their own. That
was always Katkov's way. That is why I say
that Katkov was a stupid man. Now, there is
something of the same sort in Chicherin, yet
can they be put even approximately on the
same level ?

" Though," L. N. added, " one has to respect
every one. Among the virtues the Chinese
place respect first. Simply, without any relation
to anything definite. Respect for the individual
and for the opinion of every man."

The conversation turned upon ancient languages and classical education. L. N. said :

" When I studied and read a great deal of Greek, I could easily understand almost any Greek book. I used to be at the examinations in the Lyceum, and saw that nearly always the pupil only understood what he had learnt beforehand. He did not understand new passages. And, indeed, at school for every fifty words that were learnt at least sixty-five rules were taught. In such a way one can't learn anything.

" I am always surprised how firmly all sorts of superstitions possess people. Superstitions, such as the Church, the Tsar, the army, etc., live for centuries, and people have got so accustomed to them that they are not now thought to be strange. But the superstition of classical education arose with us in Russia before my very eyes. Above all, not one of the most zealous partisans of classical education can give a single sensible argument in favour of the system." Then L. N. added :

" There is also the superstition of the possibility of a ' school ' in art. Hence all institutes and academies. The abnormal form which art takes now, however, is not the root of the evil, but one of its symptoms. When the religious conception of life changes, then art, too, will find its true methods."

L. N. returned to the Chinese virtue of 'respect,' and said :

"Often remarkable men suffer from the lack of that Chinese 'respect.' For instance, in Henry George's *Progress and Poverty* Marx's name is not mentioned at all ; and in his recently published posthumous work hardly eight lines refer to Marx, and those speak of the obscurity, complexity, and emptiness of Marx's works.

"Apropos of obscurity and complexity, they are nearly always a proof of the absence of true meaning. But there is one great exception— Kant, who wrote horribly, and yet he makes an epoch in the development of mankind. In many respects he discovered perfectly new horizons."

To-day after lunch L. N. went on horseback to Sokolniki and came back late in the evening. Nevertheless, when Mme. M. A. Maklakov and myself began to say good-bye, he said he would come with us. On the way Mme. Maklakov kept saying all the time how much she would like to live in the country. L. N. interrupted her :

"How it annoys me when people abuse the town with such exaggeration and say: To the country, to the country ! All depends on the person,—in town, too, one can be with Nature. Don't you remember," L. N. asked her, " we had an old gatekeeper, Vasili? He lived all his life in town ; in the summer he used to get up at 3 o'clock in the morning, and enjoyed his intercourse with Nature in our garden much more than country gentlemen do, who spend their evenings in the country playing cards. Besides, compared with the enormously important question of how to live one's life in the best and most moral way, the question of town or country has no value at all."

Before this L. N. said with a smile :

" I once said, but you must not talk about it, and I tell it you in secret : woman is generally so bad that the difference between a good and a bad woman scarcely exists."

Yasnaya Polyana, July 31st. I am working with N. N. Ge on the proofs of *Resurrection.* The corrections are to be inserted in the proof-sheets from L. N.'s draft copy, and two copies of the same are made. The draft copy remains here, and the fair copies are sent, one to Marx for the weekly *Niva,* and the other to Chertkov in England for the English edition.

It is an interesting, but worrying and difficult work. Throughout, instead of the one printed proof-sheet, one has to copy out afresh three or four long pages. Often L. N.'s corrections are written so closely that a magnifying glass has to be used to read them. Unless one has seen L. N.'s incredible work, the numerous passages that are rewritten, the additions and alterations, the same incident being sometimes written dozens of times over, one can have not the remotest idea of this labour.

August 2nd. I have been here from July 27th (in Yasnaya Polyana).

A queer young man, K., came to L. N., and, on my asking him what he was doing, he said that " he was the free son of air." K. told L. N. that he wanted to settle down in the country among the people.

L. N. in recounting it said :

" Of course, I did not advise him to do it. Usually nothing comes from such attempts. For instance, some very nice people, the N. N.'s, bought a small plot of land and settled like that in the country. A peasant cut down one of their trees ; they did not want to take action in the court against him, and soon, when the peasants learnt about it, they cut down the whole woods. The peasant boys stole their peas ; they were not beaten nor driven away, and then nearly the whole village came and stole all the peas, etc., etc.

" One should not, *above all*, look for new ways of life, for usually, in doing so, one's whole energy is spent on the external arrangement of life. And when all the external arrangement is over, one begins to feel bored and does nothing. Let every one first do his own work, if only it does not clash sharply with his convictions, and let him try to become better and better in his own situation, and then he will find new ways of life into the bargain. For the most part, all the external side of life must be neglected ; one should not bother about it. Do your own work."

To-day L. N. said of some one :

" He is a Tolstoian—that is, a man with convictions utterly opposed to mine."

Yesterday L. N. spoke of the process of creative work :

" I can't understand how any one can write without rewriting everything over and over again. I scarcely ever re-read my published writings, but if by chance I come across a page, it always strikes me : All this must be rewritten ; this is how I should have written it. . . .

" I am always interested to trace the moment, which comes quite early, when the public is satisfied ; and the artist thinks : They say it is good ; but it is just at this point that the real work begins ! "

To-day L. N. was not well. I went to him ; he was lying on the little sofa in the drawing-room. He told me of S. G. Verus's book on the Gospels.

" His final conclusion is the denial of Christ as a historical person. In the earliest written parts of the New Testament—in Paul's messages —there is not a single biographical fact about Christ. All the Gospels that have come down to us were composed between the second and fourth century A.D. Of the writers who were Christ's contemporaries (Tacitus, Suetonius, Philo, J. Flavius) not a single one of them mentions Christ; so that his personality is not historical, but legendary.

" All this is very interesting and even valuable, for it makes it unnecessary to quarrel any more over refuting the authenticity of the Gospel stories about the miracles ; and it proves the teaching of the Gospels to be not the words of one superman, but the sum of the wisdom of all the best moral teaching expressed by many people and at different times."

L. N. also said this to me :

" Perhaps it is because I am unwell, but at moments to-day I am simply driven to despair by everything that is going on in the world: the new form of oath, the revolting proclamation about enlisting university students in the army, the Dreyfus affair, the situation in Serbia, the horrors of the diseases and deaths in the Auerbach quicksilver works. . . . I can't make out how mankind can go on living like this, with the sight of all this horror round them!

"It always strikes me how little man is valued, even in the simplest way as a valuable and useful animal. We value a horse which can carry, but man can also make boots, work in a factory, play the piano! And 50 per cent are dying! When I used to breed merino sheep and their death-rate reached 5 per cent, I was indignant and thought the shepherd very bad. And 50 per cent of the people are dying!"

I read L. N.'s most wonderful *Father Sergius*.

Moscow, August 9th. I returned from Yasnaya in the evening of the 6th. This is what I find I have written down.

The talk turned upon the woman question. The conversation was carried on in a half-jocular tone.

L. N. said:

"Woman, as a Christian, has a right to equality. Woman, as member of the modern and perfectly pagan family, must not struggle for an impossible equality. The modern family is like a tiny little boat sailing in a storm on the vast ocean. It can keep afloat if it is ruled by *one* will. But when those in the boat begin struggling, the boat is upset, and the result is what we see now in most families. The man, however bad, is in the majority of cases the more sensible of the two. Woman is nearly always in opposition to any progress. When man wants to break with the old life and to go ahead, he nearly always meets with energetic resistance from the woman. The wife catches hold of his coat-tails and will not allow him. In woman a great evil is terribly highly developed —family egotism. It is a dreadful egotism, for it commits the greatest cruelties in the name of love; as if to say, let the whole world perish so that my Serge may be happy ! . . ."

Then L. N. recalled scenes which he had observed in Moscow :

" There issues from Minangua's a gentleman in a beaver coat, with a sad face, and after him his lady, and the porter carries boxes and helps the lady into the sledge.

" I love at times to stand near the colonnade by the great theatre and watch the ladies driving up to stop at Meriliz's. I only know of two similar sights : (1) when peasant women go to Zaseka to pick up nuts the watchmen catch them, so that sometimes they give birth out of fright, and yet they go on doing it ; and (2) so it is with ladies shopping at sales.

" And their coachmen wait in the bitter cold and talk among themselves : ' My lady must have spent five thousand to-day ! '

" I shall one day write about women. When I am quite old, and my digestion is completely out of order, and I am still looking out into the world through one eye, then I shall pop my head out and tell them: That's what you are! and disappear completely, or they would peck me to death." . . .

Doctor E. N. Maliutin was in Yasnaya. L. N. said to him :

" I can't understand the usual attitude that a doctor always serves a good cause. There is no profession that is good in itself. One may be a cobbler and be better and nicer than a doctor. Why is restoring some one to health good ? At times it is quite the opposite. Man's deeds are good, not in themselves, but because of the feelings which inspire him. That's why I do not understand the desire of women to be doctors, trained nurses, midwives, as though by becoming a midwife everything is settled for the best."

On some occasion L. N. said :

" When you are told about a complicated and difficult affair, for the most part about some one's disgusting behaviour, reply to it : Did *you* make the jam ? or : Won't you like to have tea ?— and that's all. Much harm comes from the so-called attempt to understand circumstances and relations."

October 1*st*. I came to Yasnaya Polyana yesterday. It is very nice here now the weather is mild, almost bright, but rather cold. There are no strangers. I am copying *Resurrection* again, on which L. N. is hard at work. Now I am doing the first chapters of Part III.

There is little joy in the Tolstois' family life, and to an intimate friend this is extremely marked.

Moscow, November 26*th*. I am much distressed by L. N.'s serious illness, which at the bottom of my mind I consider hopeless. I called on Wednesday to inquire after his health, and the news was very unfavourable.

December 7*th*. When Tolstoi was ill (he is much better now) and I was for the first time in his room, he seemed glad to see me, which was a great delight to me. On his table was

the volume of Tyutchev's poems. In his hand
he had an English book, *Empire and Freedom* (I
don't remember by whom). As is always his
way, Tolstoi at once spoke of what he was
reading.

" Here is a remarkable book ! " said Tolstoi.
" He (the author) is American, therefore an
Anglo-Saxon; nevertheless, he denies the so-
called civilizing influence of the Anglo-Saxon
race. I can't understand how people can stick to
such superstitions ! I understand a Muhammad
preaching his doctrine,—mediæval Christianity,
the Crusades. Whatever the convictions of those
people may have been, they did it in the belief
that they knew the truth and were giving that
knowledge to others. But now there is nothing ! Everything is done for the sake of
profit ! "

Then Tolstoi began to talk about a French
pamphlet on the workers' co-operative societies
which he had read.

" Why not introduce in the villages here
such co-operative societies ? That is a vital
thing ! You, instead of doing nothing," he
turned to Ilya Lvovich, who sat there, " ought
to do it here in the village.

" Socialist ideas have become a truism. Who
can now seriously dispute the idea that every

one should have the right to enjoy the result of his labour ? "

Then the conversation turned upon the *obschina*.

Tolstoi said :

" Everything is taken away from the peasants; they are overtaxed, oppressed in all ways. The only good thing left is the *obschina*. And then every one criticizes it and makes it responsible for all the miseries of the peasants, in their wish to take away from the peasants their last good thing. They make out that the mutual responsibility of the members is one of the evils of the *obschina*. But mutual responsibility is only one of the principles of the *obschina* with regard to fiscal purposes. If I use a good thing for an evil end, that does not prove that the thing is in itself bad."

Then the conversation turned upon Tyutchev. The other day Tolstoi saw in the *Novoe Vremya* his poem "Twilight." He therefore took down all Tyutchev's poems and read them during his illness.

Tolstoi said to me :

" I am always saying that a work of art is either so good that there is no standard by which to define its qualities—that is real art,—or it is quite bad. Now, I am happy to have found a real work of art. I cannot read it without tears. I know it by heart. Listen, I'll read it to you."

Tolstoi began in a voice broken with tears :

" The dove-coloured shadows melted together. . . ."

When I am on my death-bed I shall not forget the impression then produced on me by Tolstoi. He lay on his back, convulsively twisting the edge of his blanket with his fingers and trying in vain to restrain the tears that choked him. He broke down several times and began again. But at last, when he read the end of the stanza, "Everything is in me, and I in everything," his voice gave way. The entrance of A. N. Dunaev stopped him. He grew calmer.

" What a pity that I spoilt the poem for you!" he said to me later.

Then I played the piano.

Tolstoi asked me not to play Chopin, saying : " I am afraid I might burst into tears."

Tolstoi asked for something by Mozart or Haydn.

He asked : " Why do pianists never play Haydn ? You ought to. How good it is— beside a modern complicated, artificial work— to play something of Mozart or Haydn!"

1900

Moscow, January 29th. Tolstoi had a conversation with V. E. Den when Chalyapin was here. Tolstoi is working now on the article on the labour question, "New Slavery," and the conversation turned upon labour.

Tolstoi said : " We are going through a new stage in the evolution of slavery : the slavery of the working men suffering under the yoke of the well-to-do classes.

" Slavery will never cease at the bottom first, exclusively from the movement of the slaves themselves. We saw it in America, and here during the serfdom of the peasants. So must it happen now again. It is only when we realize that it is a shame to have slaves, that we shall cease to be slave-drivers, and shall voluntarily give up exploiting the working classes.

" Freedom cannot come from the slaves. Individual slaves who have rid themselves of the yoke of slavery become in the majority of cases particularly harsh oppressors and tyrants over their late brothers. Nor can it be otherwise. How can you expect from them—harassed and tortured—anything else? It is only when we voluntarily give up the shameful use of the labour of the slaves, our brothers, that slavery will come to an end.

" Science, in so far as it describes and clarifies the real state of things, does a useful and necessary work. But as soon as it starts laying down programmes for the future, it becomes useless. All these ideas about an eight-hour working day, etc., only increase and legalize the evil. Labour must be free, not slavish, and that is all.

" When a peasant gets up before sunrise and works all day long in the field, he is not a slave. He has intercourse with nature, he does a useful work. But when he stands by a piece of machinery in a Morosov's factory all his life long, manufacturing textiles which he will never see, and neither himself nor any one of his people will ever use, then he is a slave and perishes in slavery.

" Railways, telephones, and the other accessories of the civilized world—all that is useful and good. But if one had to choose either the whole of this civilization, for which not hundreds of thousands of ruined lives are required, but

only the certain destruction of one single existence, or, on the other hand, no civilization at
all, then no thank you for this civilization with
its railways and telephones, if a necessary condition of them is the destruction of human life."

February 24th. On the 18th and 20th I was
at the Tolstois'. On the 18th Tolstoi went to
the " Pod Deviche " playhouse and afterwards
to a dirty public-house, where there is an extraordinary amount of drunkenness and debauchery,
to make observations.

Tolstoi said :

" Twenty years ago I saw at the ' Pod
Deviche,' *Churkin*, a play composed by a drunken
tramp, and this time I saw *Stenka Rasin*—and
it is all the same thing. Murder and violence
are represented as heroic and are acclaimed by
the crowd. And it is remarkable that whilst
every word in a book which may enlighten the
minds of the people is carefully struck out by the
censorship, such performances are readily allowed,
under the police inspector's censorship. During
the last twenty years probably over a million
people have seen these *Churkins* and *Rasins*."

In telling this, Tolstoi recollected how he was
once in a workhouse where the priest explained
the Gospels :

" The passage was read where Christ says :
' It is said : thou shalt not kill ; but I say unto
you, do not be angry without cause.' The
priest began to explain that one must not be
angry without cause, but, if the authorities
become angry, that is right and as it should be.
' Do not kill ' also does not mean that one should
never kill. In war or at an execution, killing
is necessary and is not a sin. This is the only
chance that an illiterate person has to understand the meaning of the Gospels, for in church
all the chapters are either indistinctly read by the
sexton, or shouted so loud that they are perfectly
unintelligible—and this is the way in which the
Gospels are explained to the people ! "

A long talk about the Boers and the English
took place.

Tolstoi said :

" I always consider that moral motives are
effective and decisive historically. And now,
when the universal dislike of the English is so
clearly pronounced—I shall not live to see it,
but it seems to me that the power of England
will be much shaken. And I say this not out
of an unconscious Russian patriotism. If Poland
or Finland rose against Russia and success were
on their side, my sympathy would be on their
side as the oppressed.

" The Russian people, speaking impartially, is perhaps the most Christian of all in its moral character. It is partly to be explained by the fact that the Gospels have been read by the Russian people for nine hundred years ; Catholics don't know the Gospels even now, and other races came to know the Gospel only after the Reformation.

" I was struck when I saw in the streets of London a criminal escorted by the police, and the police had to protect him energetically from the crowd, which threatened to tear him to pieces. With us it is just the opposite : police have to drive away by force the people who try to give the criminal money and bread. With us, criminals and prisoners are ' little unhappy ones.' But now, unfortunately, there is a change for the worse, and our abominable Government tries with all its might and main to rouse hatred against the condemned. In Siberia, even prizes are given to any one who kills an escaped prisoner."

April 29*th*. The conversation was on Shakespeare. Tolstoi is not very fond of him. Tolstoi said :

" Three times in my life I have read through Shakespeare and Goethe from end to end, and

I could never make out in what their charm consisted."

According to Tolstoi, Goethe is cold. Among his (Goethe's) works he likes many of the lyrics and *Hermann and Dorothea*. He does not like Goethe's dramatic works, and his novels he considers quite weak. Tolstoi did not speak about *Faust*.

Tolstoi is very fond of Schiller, and said: " He is a genuine man ! " He loves almost all his works, particularly *The Robbers* and *Don Carlos*, also *Mary Stuart*, *William Tell*, and *Wallenstein*.

Then A. M. Sukhotin, a man over seventy, read aloud Turgenev's *Old Portraits* superbly. Tolstoi did not remember the story, and was in great delight over it. He said :

" It is only after reading all these moderns that one really appreciates Turgenev."

Tolstoi remembered Turgenev with great love. He said, in passing :

" When Turgenev died I wanted to read a paper about him. I wanted especially, in view of the misunderstandings that there had been between us, to remember and relate all the good that was so abundant in him, and to tell what I loved in him. The lecture was not given. Dolgorukov did not allow it."

The conversation turned on Chekhov and Gorky. Tolstoi as usual praised Chekhov's artistic gift very highly. The lack of a definite world conception grieves him in Chekhov ; and in this respect Tolstoi prefers Gorky. Of Gorky Tolstoi said :

" You know what he is from his works. Gorky's great and very serious essential defect is a poorly developed sense of proportion, and this is extremely important. I pointed out this defect to Gorky himself, and as an instance I drew his attention to his misuse of the method of animating inanimate things. Then Gorky said that in his opinion it was a good method, and gave an instance of it in his story *Malva*, where it says : ' the sea laughed.' I replied to him that, if on certain occasions the method might be very successful, nevertheless one ought not to abuse it."

Yesterday Ushakov asked Tolstoi about Gromeka. Tolstoi and Tatyana Lvovna spoke a great deal about him.

Tolstoi said :

" He was a sympathetic, passionate, and gifted man. He shot himself when still a young man, it was said because he was mentally deranged."

Tatyana Lvovna says, by the way, that

Gromeka was her first admirer and proposed to her when she was sixteen.

Tolstoi values Gromeka's criticism very much. He said :

" It was a pleasure to me that a man who sympathized with me could see *even* in *War and Peace* and in *Anna Karenin* a great deal of what I was afterwards to say and write."

Tolstoi also said :

" When I wrote the story *What Men Live by*, Fet said, ' Well, what do people live by ? By money, of course.' "

I observed that Fet had probably said it in joke. Tolstoi replied :

" No, it was his conviction. And, as often happens, what people try very stubbornly to get, they do get. Fet all his life long wanted to become rich, and he became rich. His brothers and sisters, it seems, went out of their minds, and all their fortunes came to him."

Fet wrote in Tatyana Lvovna's album that the unhappiest day of his life was the one when he saw that he was going to be ruined.

I talked a good deal with Tolstoi to-day. Tolstoi said about current events :

" I am not so much horrified at these murders in the Transvaal, and now in China, as by the open declaration of immoral motives. They used at least to cloak themselves hypocritically in good motives, but now that this is no longer possible they express all their immoral and cruel intentions and claims openly."

We spoke about the abolition of deportation. Tolstoi considers it worse than the other method. He said :

" Instead of making it possible for a man to order his life in a new place, he is put into prison. The Government has already voted six and a half millions for the enlargement of prisons. And this money will again be flayed off the peasants, for there is nowhere else to take it from."

Of our courts of justice Tolstoi said :

" How absurd our courts are can be seen at each stage. For example, take the case of the Tula priest. How was it that the Tula court acquitted him, and then after the acquittal the Oriol court sentenced him to hard labour for twenty years ? If such uncertainty is possible, what are those verdicts worth ? Indeed, it depends on a thousand accidents : the temper of the jurymen, the behaviour of the prisoner at the bar—the prisoner bursts into tears, and the impression produced secures his acquittal. It is merely a game of heads and tails ! It would be simpler and easier to say : Heads or tails, and to give sentence accordingly. It simply baffles me how decent people can be judges ! "

Of the case of S. I. Mamontov, Tolstoi said :

" One is certainly very sorry for him : he is an old, unhappy man ; but, on the other hand, you have to remember that the man has squandered twelve millions, or whatever it may be ; he certainly spent between one and two hundred thousand roubles per annum, and is then acquitted, while another wretched man steals a trifle and is condemned for it. And in his case, too, money was spent on expensive lawyers. This reminds me of the anecdote I read in the papers. A cashier who embezzled twenty-five thousand roubles came to a lawyer to ask him to undertake his defence. The lawyer asked him : ' Is there any more money left ? ' The cashier said that there was another twenty-five thousand. Then the lawyer said : ' Take the rest and give it to me, and then I will undertake your case.'

" And why should the jury be able to pardon ? Only the plaintiff can pardon ; but the jury whom he has not hurt have nothing to pardon him for.

" I once talked to N. V. Davidov, and said to him that all punishment may be dispensed with, yet an enquiry ought to be made ; and when the crime is proved, they should go to the criminal and accuse him in the presence of all of his crime, and should bring forward the proof of his guilt. It is quite likely that the man will say : ' Be damned to you, it is none of your business ! ' But still I think that this method would more often give positive results than the existing system of punishment."

Speaking of the Government, Tolstoi said :

" I wonder why they have not put me into prison yet ? Particularly now, after my article on ' Patriotism.' Perhaps they have not read it yet ? It ought to be sent to them."

Tolstoi spoke again of his indifference to modern complicated music :

" I tried to accustom myself to modern dissonances, but these are all a perversion of taste. A modern composer takes a musical idea, now and then even a lovely one, and twists it round and round without end or measure, combines it with other themes, and, when at last he manages to express something simple, one is ready to heave a sigh of relief and say : Thank God ! "

July 4th. Yesterday Tolstoi said to me :

" Buddha says that happiness consists in doing as much good as possible to others. However strange this may seem on the face of it, yet it is true without a doubt : happiness is only possible when the struggle for personal happiness is renounced."

Then Tolstoi smiled and said :

" And yet you play the piano ! But certainly that is better than many other things. At any rate you need not pass sentence on any one, or commit murder."

Tolstoi said of newspapers :

" At present the newspaper infection has reached its ultimate limits. All the questions of the day are artificially puffed up by the newspapers. The worst danger is that the newspapers present everything ready made, without making people stop to think about anything. A liberal Kuzminsky, or even a Koni, takes his fresh newspaper with his morning coffee, reads it, goes to his court, where he meets others who have just read the very same newspaper, and the contagion is spread ! "

Tolstoi went on to say :

" It has suddenly become perfectly clear to me that the evil lies in regulations, *i.e.* the chief thing is not that people do wrong, but that some force others to do a wrong which is considered to be right. Hitherto not a single one even of the most extreme socialist doctrines has dispensed with compulsion. But slavery will only cease when every one is free to choose his work and the time needed for it.

"People always put an end to things by asking : 'Well ; let us suppose that we have liberated the slave, what will follow next ? How is it going to be done?' I do not know how it is going to be done, but I do know that the existing order is the greatest evil, and therefore I must try to take as little part as possible in keeping it going. But what will come in place of that evil—I do not and must not know. For what reason did we, the well-to-do classes, take upon ourselves the rôle of the controllers of life ? Let the freed slaves arrange things for themselves. I know only this, that it is bad to be a slave and worse still to own slaves, and therefore I must rid myself of the evil. That's all."

Tolstoi wanted to take for the motto of his new book, *The Slavery of our Times*, Marx's saying that since the capitalists made themselves masters of the working classes the European governments lost all shame.

Tolstoi praised Elzbacher's book on anarchy, in which the doctrines of seven anarchists are expounded : of Godwin, Proudhon, Max Stirner, Bakunin, Kropotkin, B. P. Tucker, and Tolstoi himself.

Tolstoi said :

" I myself can remember at the beginning of the socialist movement in Russia that the word ' socialist ' was only spoken in a whisper ; but when Professor Ivanyukov in the first years of the eighties openly wrote his book on socialism, it was already a widely spread doctrine in Western Europe. It is in the same way that the public now regard anarchism, often crudely identifying this doctrine with the throwing of bombs."

Of Elzbacher's book Tolstoi said :

" At the end of the book is an alphabetical index of the words used by the seven anarchists. It appears that the word *Zwang*, compulsion, violence, is absent only in the exposition of my views."

Sergeenko was telling Tolstoi about Volinsky's book on Leonardo da Vinci, and said it was a fine book.

Tolstoi remarked :

" Yes, it seems to be one of those books which are good in that it is not necessary to read them."

Tolstoi said yesterday about doctors and science generally :

" How trivial and unnecessary are all our sciences ! It is true that exact sciences—mathematics and chemistry, although quite unimportant for the improvement of moral life, are at any rate exact and positive. But, although medical science has a great deal of knowledge, that amount is nothing in proportion to what is needed in order actually to know anything. And what is the good of it ? "

I replied to Tolstoi that, although in theory it may be so, yet in practice, when some one is ill, one always wants to help them.

To this Tolstoi replied :

" It often happens that if some one is seriously ill, those around him, at the bottom of their hearts, want him to die, in order to be rid of him —he is in their way."

Tolstoi said to Sophie Andreevna :

" It's time for us to die," and he quoted Pushkin's lines :

" And then our heir in a lucky moment will crush us down with a heavy monument."

July 5th. Tolstoi went for a walk to-day with myself and P. A. Sergeenko. We passed through the splendid young fir-tree forest on the left of the road to Kozlovka.

Tolstoi said :

" I am trying to like and appreciate the modern writers, but it is so difficult. Dostoevsky often wrote so badly, so weakly and incompetently, from the point of view of technique; but what a lot he always has to say! Taine said that for one page of Dostoevsky's he would give all French novels.

"And technique has now reached a wonderful perfection. A Mme. Lukhmanov or Mme. D. writes quite wonderfully. What are Turgenev or myself compared with her! She could give us forty points' start of her!"

Tolstoi has recently re-read all Chekhov's short stories. To-day he said of Chekhov:

"His mastery is of the highest order. I have been re-reading his stories with the greatest pleasure. Some, as, for instance, 'Children,' 'Sleepy,' 'In Court,' are real masterpieces. I really read one story after another with great pleasure. And yet it is all a mosaic; there is no connecting inner link.

"The most important thing in a work of art is that it should have a kind of focus, *i.e.* there should be some place where all the rays meet or from which they issue. And this focus must not be able to be completely explained in words. This indeed is one of the significant facts about a true work of art—that its content in its entirety can be expressed only by itself."

Tolstoi finds a great likeness between the talents of Chekhov and Maupassant. He prefers

Maupassant for his greater joy in life. But, on the other hand, Chekhov's gift is a purer gift then Maupassant's.

Sergeenko, I don't remember in what connection, recalled a poem by Lermontov.

Tolstoi said:

"He had indeed a permanent and powerful seeking after truth! Pushkin has not that moral significance, but the sense of beauty is developed in him more highly than in any one else. In Chekhov, and in modern writers generally, there is an extraordinary development of the technique of realism. In Chekhov everything is real to the verge of illusion. His stories give the impression of a stereoscope. He throws words about in apparent disorder, and, like an impressionist painter, he achieves wonderful results by his touches."

Tolstoi likes M. Gorky very much as a man. He begins, however, to be disappointed with his work.

Tolstoi said of him:

"Gorky lacks a sense of proportion. He has a familiar style which is unpleasant."

Tolstoi wrote a short preface to Von Polenz's novel *Der Büttnerbauer*.

On that occasion he said:

"As I read the novel, I kept saying to myself:

'Why did not you, you fool, write this novel?'—indeed, I know this world ; and how very important it is to point out the poetry of peasant life! Men with their civilization will cut down this lime tree here, this forest; they will lay pavements and make houses with tall chimneys, and they will destroy the boundless beauty of natural life."

On my asking him whether he had ever tried to write such a novel, Tolstoi said that he had done so several times long ago.

Tolstoi said of Grigorovich :

" He is now old-fashioned and seems feeble, but he is an important and remarkable writer, and God grant that Chekhov may be a tenth part as important as Grigorovich was. He belonged to the number of the best men who found an important movement. He has also many artistic merits. For instance, in the beginning of his *Anton Goremika*, when the old peasant comes home and gives his son or grandson a twig, it is a moving incident which depicts the old peasant as well as the simplicity and artlessness of his life."

Of Turgenev, Tolstoi said :

" He was a typical representative of the men of the 'fifties—a radical in the best sense of the word. His struggle against serfdom is remarkable, and also his love for what he describes;

for instance, the way he describes the old man in *Old Portraits*. And then there is his sensitiveness to the beauties of nature."

Speaking of the province of criticism, Tolstoi said:

"The value of criticism consists in pointing out all the good that there is in this or that work of art, and in thus directing the opinion of the public, whose tastes are mostly crude and the majority of whom have no feeling for beauty. Just as it is difficult to be a really good critic, so it is easy for the most stupid and limited man to become a critic; and as good critics are needed, so bad critics are merely harmful. It is a particularly absurd and cheap habit of critics to express, in talking of other people's work, all sorts of personal ideas which have nothing to do with the book they are criticizing. This is the most useless gossip."

July 7th. Tolstoi said that all human vices can be reduced to three classes: (1) anger, malevolence; (2) vanity; and (3) lust—in the widest sense of the word. The last is the most powerful.

In the morning, at coffee, Tolstoi sighed and said:

"Yes, it is hard, it is hard. . . . It is hard because falsehood and arrogance prevail in the higher ranks of society, and because there is much darkness among the people. The other day two sectarians of the priestless sect came to me from Tula: one a young one, evidently of little understanding, and the other an old man, who, while we talked, kept putting on his spectacles. The old man turned out to be understanding, wise, and said many things to the point, as though he agreed with my religious views; and yet when I offered them tea they refused because they had not brought their tea things with them."

On the occasion of the Boxer rising Tolstoi said:

"It is terrible that it should happen in such an awful way. But, although it is difficult to foresee, yet it is to be expected that after the war a greater understanding will take place between Europeans and the Chinese; and I think that the Chinese are bound to have a most beneficial influence on us, if only because of their extraordinary capacity for work and of their ability to grow more on a small plot of land and obtain better results than we do on a space a dozen times larger."

Tolstoi compares the present state of Europe with the end of the Roman Empire. The Chinese, in his opinion, play the part of the "barbarians."

Tolstoi said to-day :

" All our actions are divided into those which have a value, and those which have no value at all, in the face of death. If I were told that I had to die to-morrow, I should not go out for a ride on horseback ; but if I were about to die this moment, and Levochka here" (Leo Lvovich's son, who passed across the terrace at that moment with his nurse) " fell and burst into tears, I should run to him and pick him up. We are all in the position of passengers from a ship which has reached an island. We have gone on shore, we walk about and gather shells, but we must always remember that, when the whistle sounds, all the little shells will have to be thrown away and we must run to the boat."

Sophie Andreevna, who was present during some of the talks, argued all the time, and answered Tolstoi in a very feminine way. When Sophie Andreevna on a walk said that a woman, while her husband writes novels and philosophical articles, has to bear, to give birth to, and to rear her children, and how difficult all this is, Tolstoi became indignant and exclaimed with a bitterness that was rare in him :

" What terrible things you are saying, Sonechka ! A woman who is annoyed at having children and does not desire them is not a woman, but a whore ! "

In the evening we sat on the balcony : Tolstoi, Sergeenko, and myself.

Tolstoi wondered at the illogicality of women, and turning to me said :

" Peter Alexeevich and myself have a right to speak about women, but you have none. One must have a wife and daughters to do this. Daughters are perhaps the more important of the two. Daughters are the only women who are not ' women ' at all to a man, and who can be known fully from the beginning. With sisters such a relation is impossible, for one grows up side by side with them ; a certain rivalry enters into the relation, and one cannot know one's sister, entirely, as a whole."

Sergeenko asked Tolstoi's advice as to how to educate his son sexually.

Tolstoi said to him :

" These questions are so dangerous that it is better that parents should not speak of them at all to their children. It is only necessary to watch the influence of surroundings. At times a vicious boy, or one who is not vicious at all, but spoilt in this sense, can corrupt a whole circle of boys. It is best of all that a growing boy should be as much as possible among young girls. But there are among modern girls some that are worse than young men. If a feeling of romance is felt for any girl, this is the best protection against immorality. . . ."

July 12th. Yesterday I returned home. On the day of my departure during our walk Sophie Andreevna was talking about the sale of the Samara estate, which she has completed for four hundred and fifty thousand roubles (Tolstoi originally bought the estate cheap), and by the sale of which Andrey, Michael, and Alexandra will get 150,000 roubles each. This money was the topic of conversation during the last few days, and how the sons meant to buy this or some other estate. At the end of the walk Tolstoi and myself found ourselves ahead of the others. Suddenly he gave a heavy sigh.

I asked him : " Why do you sigh, Leo Nikolaevich ? "

" If you knew how painful it is to me to hear it all ! I have it always on my conscience that I, with my wish to renounce property, once bought estates. It is funny to think that it seems now as if I had wished to make provision for my children, and in doing so I did them the greatest injury. Look at my Andryusha. He is completely incapable of doing anything, and lives on the people whom I once robbed and whom my children keep on robbing. How terrible it is to listen to all this talk now, to watch it all going on! It is so opposed to my ideas and desires and to everything I live by. . . . Oh! that they would spare me! . . ."

Tolstoi was silent for a time, and then said :

" Why did I suddenly begin complaining ? "

At that moment Tatyana Lvovna came up, and our conversation turned on other subjects.

Tolstoi talked about poetry.

" When a poem deals with love, flowers, etc., it is a comparatively innocent occupation until the age of sixteen. But to express in verse an important and serious idea without distorting the idea is almost impossible. How very difficult it is to express one's thoughts by words only, so that every one understands just what you want to express! How much more difficult, then, it is when the writer is bound by metre and rhyme! Only the very great poets have succeeded in doing it, and rarely too. Perfectly false ideas are often hidden behind verses."

An undergraduate who had written an article upon Tolstoi in reply to Nordau's criticism came, and turned out to be a foolish young man.

Tolstoi had been unwell for the last few days and in a bad temper, so that he came to us quite upset and said :

" No, it is time, it is time for me to die ! They stick to some single idea, which they arbitrarily choose from the rest, and go on and on repeating : Non-resistance ! non-resistance ! How am I to blame for it ? "

Sophie Andreevna said to me :

" The private life of famous men is always distorted in their biographies. They are sure to make me out a Xantippe. You must take my side, Alexander Borisovich ! " . . .

During our walk Sophie Andreevna showed me the spot which is called "the apiary," and said :

" There actually was an apiary here once. Leo N. was at one time mad about bees, and used to spend whole days in the apiary. We often drove here, taking a samovar and having tea here. Once Fet came here, and we went to join Leo N. at the apiary. It was a wonderful evening ; we sat here for a long time ; and there were many glow-worms in the grass. Leo N. said to me : ' Now, Sonia, you always wanted emerald earrings ; take two glow-worms for earrings.' Thereupon Fet wrote a poem in which were these lines :

In my hand is thy hand—what a marvel !
On the ground are two glow-worms, two emeralds."

At another point Sophie Andreevna showed me the field where Tolstoi and Turgenev once stood when shooting, and she was with them.

Sophie Andreevna said :

" It was the last time Turgenev stayed at Yasnaya, not long before his death. I asked him : 'Ivan Sergeevich, why don't you write now ?' He answered : 'In order to write I had always to be a little in love. Now I am old, I can't fall in love any more, and that is why I have stopped writing.'"

December 27th. Last night I was at the Tolstois'. There were Tolstoi, Ilya, and Andrey (Tolstoi's sons). A message arrived that Tatyana Lvovna had given birth prematurely to a still-born child ; a day before, news reached Yasnaya Polyana that the son of Leo Lvovich, a boy of about two, was dead. Sophie Andreevna left for Yasnaya. There was an atmosphere of depression.

Tolstoi played chess with me. Later P. S. Usov came, who also played a game of chess with Tolstoi. We began to talk. Tolstoi became animated. The post arrived. There were three letters from Chertkov. In one of them

there were many pages of closely written manuscript.

Tolstoi glanced at it and said :

" It is probably a woman's writing. How
nice it would be if one need not read it ! "

The manuscript, however, turned out not to
be from a woman, so that Tolstoi put it aside
to read it.

Referring to his daughter's misfortune, Tolstoi
said :

" I am not sorry that my daughters have no
children ; I cannot be glad that I have grand-
children. I know that they will inevitably grow
up to be idlers. My daughters are certainly
anxious that this should not be so, but considering the surroundings in which they will have to
be brought up, it is very difficult to avoid it. All
my life long I have had these surroundings, and,
however much I struggle, I can do nothing.
Now, during the Christmas season I can't bear
to look at this mad extravagance ; these visits.
What a terrible absurdity it is ! "

Usov was saying in what circumstances a
doctor has the right to bring on birth artificially,
thereby killing the baby.

Tolstoi replied :

" It is always immoral. For the most part,
when there are various ways of relieving the

patient, oxygen, etc., it is difficult to abstain from using them; but it would be better if they did not exist. We shall all die without fail, and the doctors' activity is directed towards fighting death. But to die—in ten days or in ten years—is all the same. How terrible it is that it is always concealed from the patient that he is dying! We are none of us accustomed to look death in the face!"

Usov defended the activity of doctors, considering it a useful one.

Tolstoi said:

"It is for this reason that I consider the activity of doctors harmful: people are crowded in towns; they are infected with syphilis and consumption; they are kept in terrible conditions, and then millions are spent on the establishment of hospitals and clinics. But why not spend that energy, not in curing people, but in improving the conditions of their lives? While numbers of healthy, useful peasants are infected with all sorts of diseases, and are worn out by work beyond their strength, so that they die at thirty instead of seventy, some useless old woman who is quite incurable has spent upon her all the treatment that medicine can supply.

"All modern sciences do the very opposite of what they set out to do. Theology hides moral truths, jurisprudence obscures in every possible way the conception of justice, the natural sciences teach materialism, and history distorts the true life of the people. Darwin's theory is in agreement with the crude fable of Moses. All discussions on Darwinism are polemics against Moses.

" Every young man growing up in Russia passes through a terrible contagion, a sort of moral syphilis ; in the first place, the Orthodox Church, and then, when he frees himself from that, the doctrines of materialism. The best physiologists, like Krafft-Ebing or Claude Bernard, openly admit that, however carefully we investigate even a simple cell, there is always some x in its composition which we do not understand. Consequently the complex of organisms and the social conditions of life are an x raised to the x degree. And if we cannot investigate a cell completely, then how can we realize the laws which govern the life of human societies ? Yet some blockhead like B. assures us that it is all very simple, and the science of history can deduce immutable laws by which human life is shaped.

" Look at all our historians : what dull, stupid men they are ! For instance, Solovev. He was an incredibly dull man. And when some one

gifted appears among them—a Granovsky, Kosto-
marov, Kudryavzev—and you ask, 'What after
all have they done?' it turns out that they have
done nothing of any importance or value. Take
Kluchevsky, for instance: what has he done?
He talks brilliantly, toys with the liberal point
of view about Catherine the Great, and says
that she was a whore—well, we knew that
without him. Or take the man who dances
the mazurka in the Moscovskya Vedomsti,
Ilovaisky—he is an historian too!

"What should be taught at school? Long
ago, when I was interested in education, I came
to the conclusion that school teaching ought to
consist of two branches only, of languages and
mathematics. This is the only positive knowledge that one can give a pupil. There is no
humbug about this. Either you know it or
you don't know it. Besides, from this fundamental knowledge all science can develop. From
mathematics come astronomy, physics, natural
sciences. From languages, history, geography,
and so on. But with us, who is taught and what
are they taught? To-day I walked in the street.
Drunken men were going about, swearing
obscenely, dragging women after them. Who
has ever said a single word to these men about
their moral needs? What did we teach them?

" The other evening I was coming home from the Turkish bath and walked near the theatres. Policemen on horseback were lounging about; coachmen with buttocks like this " (Tolstoi illustrated it with his hands) " and rows of buttons on their backs sit on the boxes. And in the illuminated theatres, crowded with people, a divine service is performed: a silly and distorted story *Sadko* (an opera) is acted, or ' When we dead awaken ' is played. It's sheer madness ! "

1901

Moscow, February 1st. Tolstoi began about a couple of months ago to learn Dutch, and now he reads quite easily, at the age of seventy-three !

He has an original way of learning languages : he gets the New Testament in the language he wants to know, and whilst reading it through he learns the language.

Tolstoi said to me recently about modern art :

" The sense of shame is lost. I cannot call it anything else—the sense of æsthetic shame. I wonder if you know the feeling ? I feel it most strongly when I read something that is artistically false, and I can call it nothing else but shame."

With regard to his play, *The Corpse*, Tolstoi said to me :

" The son of the wife of the man I described came to me, and then the man himself. The son on behalf of his mother asked me not to publish the play,[1] because it would be very painful to her, and also because she was afraid of the consequences. I of course promised.

" Their visit was very interesting and useful to me. Once more, as so many times before, I was convinced how much feebler and more unreal are the psychological motives which one invents oneself in order to explain actions. The actions of one's imaginary characters are then the motives which guided those people in real life. After talking to these people I cooled to my work."

On another occasion, in the dining-room downstairs, animated conversation was going on among the younger people. Tolstoi, who was resting in the next room in the dark, afterwards came into the dining-room and said to me :

" I lay there and listened to your talk. It interested me from two points of view : it was interesting simply to hear young people talking, and then it was also interesting from the dramatic

[1] The theme of *The Corpse* became known to the newspapers through Tolstoi's copyist, Alexander Petrovich, who, in a drunken bout in the Khitrovka, told a fellow drunkard, a reporter of the *Novosti Dnya*, that Tolstoi was writing a play, and also told him the subject of the play. The reporter made an article of it and published it in the paper. This was the cause of the *dramatis personae* coming to Tolstoi, and it was also one of the reasons why Tolstoi left the play unfinished. (Years afterwards the play, finished, was published and entitled *The Living Corpse*.)

point of view. I listened and said to myself: This is how one ought to write for the stage. It is not one speaking and the others listening. It is never like that. It is necessary that all should speak, and the art of the writer consists in making what he wants run through it like a beautiful thread."

March 8*th*. Yesterday Tolstoi was in good form. At tea he laughed and joked. The conversation was about luxury.

Tolstoi said :

" How much more money people spend nowadays than they used ! When Sophie Andreevna and I lived in Yasnaya, our income from the Nikolsky estate was about five thousand roubles and we lived superbly. I remember when Sophie Andreevna bought little mats to lay by the beds, it seemed to me a useless and incredible luxury. And now my sons—I seem to have about twenty of them—squander money right and left, buy dogs, horses, gramophones. I asked myself then, why buy carpets when we have slippers ? Certainly we did not go barefoot, but, behold, Riepin painted me *décolleté*, barefooted, in a shirt ! I have to thank him for not having taken off my nether garments ! And he never asked me, if I liked it ! But I have long since got used to being treated as if I were dead. There, in the Peredvizhni exhibition, you will see the Devil (Riepin's ' Temptation of Christ '), and you'll also see the man possessed by the Devil ! "

On February 25th Tolstoi's excommunication was announced. That day Tolstoi and A. N. Dunaev went on some business to a doctor and came into the Lubiansky Square. In the square, by the fountain, the crowd recognized Tolstoi. At first, as Dunaev relates, an ironical voice was heard : " Here's the Devil in the likeness of a man ! " This served for a signal. The crowd threw themselves like one man on Tolstoi. All shouted and threw up their hats. Tolstoi was confused ; he didn't know what to do and walked away almost at a run. The crowd followed him. With great difficulty Tolstoi and Dunaev managed to get a sledge at the corner of Neglinny. The crowd wanted to stop the cabman and many held on to the sledge. At that moment a troop of mounted police appeared, let the cab through, and immediately made a ring and cut off the crowd.

On the occasion of his excommunication Tolstoi received, and is still receiving, a number of addresses, letters of sympathy, etc. One lady sent him a piece of holy bread and a letter in which she said that she had just received the

Sacrament and took the Host for his benefit. She ends her letter : " Eat it in health and pay no heed to these stupid priests."

August 9th. I was the other day in Yasnaya Polyana. Tolstoi is hale and hearty. I have not seen him like that for a long time.

The conversation was about Russian writers.

Tolstoi said :

" I was fond of Turgenev as a man. As a writer, I do not attribute particular importance to him or to Goncharov. Their subjects, the number of ordinary characters and love scenes, have too ephemeral an importance. If I were asked which of the Russian writers I consider the most important, I would say : Pushkin, Lermontov, Gogol, Hertzen, whom our Liberals have forgotten, and Dostoevsky, whom they do not read at all. Well, and then : Griboedov, Ostrovsky, Tyutchev."

Of Gogol's works Tolstoi does not like *Taras Bulba* at all. He far prefers *The Revisor* (*Inspector General*), *Dead Souls*, *Shinel*, *Koliaska* ("it's a masterpiece in miniature"), *Nevsky Prospect*. Of Pushkin's works, he considers *Boris Godunov* a failure.

It is characteristic that in making his selection Tolstoi said :

" I do not speak of myself; it's not for me, but for others, to judge of my importance."

That evening in his study Tolstoi said to me : "Alexander Borisovich, an image comes before me. Rays spread out from a centre. The centre is the spiritual essence ; the rays are the perpetually growing needs of the body. A time comes when a spiritual life begins to exist inside these rays. They spread out at an ever diminishing angle, become parallel, and at last draw together and finally unite in the one infinitely small and entirely spiritual centre—death."

Gaspra, Crimea. September 12th. Chekhov was here yesterday. He does not look well ; he looks old and coughs perpetually. He speaks little, in short sentences, but they are always to the point. He gave a touching account of his life with his mother in the winter at Yalta. Tolstoi was very glad to see him.

Gaspra, Crimea. September 16th. Life here goes on very quietly.
After dinner I or N. L. Obolensky, or both in turn, read Chekhov's stories aloud, which Tolstoi greatly enjoys. The other day I read *The Tedious Story*. Tolstoi was in constant

raptures over Chekhov's understanding. He also liked, for the originality of the idea and the mastery of the writing, *The Bet*, and particularly *The Steppe*.

Of Chekhov Tolstoi said :

" He is a strange writer : he throws words about as if at random, and yet everything is alive. And what understanding ! He never has any superfluous details ; every one of them is either necessary or beautiful."

September 20th. I told Tolstoi about the article in the *Moscow Courier* where Maeterlinck's is quoted as saying that *Power of Darkness* is in his opinion almost the greatest play.

Tolstoi laughed and said :

" Why doesn't he imitate it, then ? "

1902

Moscow, January 13th. Tolstoi once told me :
" When I went to see *Power of Darkness* acted
I sat in the gallery on purpose so as not to be
recognized. Yet I was recognized ; they began
to tell me to go on the stage, and I hurried
home at once. But there was a moment when
I could hardly restrain myself from stepping
on to the stage and beginning to speak, to say
everything—whatever that may be."

January 15th. Gorky read aloud to Tolstoi the
end of Mazzini's book *On the Duties of Man,*
which Tolstoi likes very much. While Gorky
was reading, Tolstoi, who had read the book
more than once, was almost moved to tears.

Madame N. N. Den told me the following
story, which she had from her sister. When
Tolstoi was very ill he thought he was dying, and
took leave and said good-bye to all who were
present. Leo Lvovich was the only one of
Tolstoi's children who was absent, and Tolstoi

dictated a letter to him. Those who read it say that this farewell letter at the point of death was deeply moving. The letter, however, was not sent, for Leo Lvovich arrived at Gaspra in person. When he came into Tolstoi's room, Tolstoi said that it was difficult for him to speak, but that he had expressed all his thoughts and feelings in the letter, which he handed to his son. Leo Lvovich read the letter at once in Tolstoi's room, then came into the next room, and, in the presence of all those who were there (Countess Sophie Nicolaevna included), tore his dying father's letter into little bits and threw it in the wastepaper basket. . . .

Yasnaya Polyana, July 25th. I have been here a few days. Tolstoi is well physically.

To-day Tolstoi said to Doctor Butkevich:
✳ " The only true way for a man to improve human life is by the way of moral perfection in his personal life. Spiritual life is a constant progress, a constant effort towards the realization of truth."

The conversation turned upon literature. It began with my saying that Sienkewicz's novel, *The Sword Bearers,* was a boring book.

Tolstoi said:
" Yes, for some reason I began it, but I could

not read it. Do you remember how, when one is a child, one sometimes gets a piece of meat which one chews and chews and chews, and one can't deal with it, and at last one quietly spits it out and throws it under the table."

Then Tolstoi remembered B.'s story which he read recently :

" It begins with a superb description of nature—a little shower, which is done as Turgenev even could not do it, let alone myself. And then there is a girl. She dreams of him " (Tolstoi shortly told the plot of the story), " and all this—the girl's silly emotion, the little shower —all this is needed, in order that B. may write a story. Just as in ordinary life, when people have nothing to say they talk about the weather, so writers, when they have nothing to write about, write about the weather, and it is time to put an end to it. Yes, there was a little shower ; there might just as well have been no shower at all. I think that all this must come to an end in literature. It is simply impossible to read any longer.

"I once belonged to the guild of authors, and from habit I watch and am interested in everything that goes on there."

Tolstoi quoted a few instances of misstatements and inaccuracies in writers like Uspensky and Korolenko, but said that these were only slips. But when psychological mistakes are made, when the characters in novels and stories do what, from their spiritual nature, they cannot do, it is a terrible failing, and the works of the Andreevs, etc., are full of such mistakes. Even in Gorky it is always happening. For instance, it is the case in his story about the silver clasps, or in the opinions of the women in *Three*. His *Burghers* is utterly uninteresting. The surroundings are indefinite, untypical; nobody can make anything of it at all.

"I am always afraid of falling into the old man's habit of being unable to appreciate or to understand the present. But I try my best and genuinely can find no beauty in the modern tendencies of art. There has recently appeared a very just article by E. Markov on Gorky. The writer, rather timidly—for Gorky has become such an idol that people dare not speak of him—has pointed out correctly that modern Russian literature has completely turned away from those high moral problems which it formerly pursued. And indeed what a complete denial of moral principles there is! You may be vicious, you may rob or kill; there is nothing to restrain the individual; all is allowed. . . .

"But still I am impressed by the fact that

Gorky is translated in Europe and greatly read there. Undoubtedly there is something new in him. His chief merit is that he was the first to draw the world of outcasts and tramps from the life, which until then no one had attempted. In this respect he did what Turgenev and Grigorovich did in their day for the world of peasants.

"I love Chekhov very much and value his writings, but I could not make myself read his play, *The Three Sisters*. What is it all for? Generally speaking, modern writers have lost the conception of drama. Drama, instead of telling us the whole of a man's life, must place him in such a situation, tie such a knot, that, when it is untied, the whole man is made visible. Now, I allowed myself to criticize Shakespeare. But with him every character is alive ; and it is always clear why he acts as he does. In Shakespeare's theatre there were boards with inscriptions ' moonlight,' ' a house,' because (Heaven be praised !) the whole attention was concentrated on the substance of the drama. Now it is just the opposite."

Tolstoi spoke with disgust of Andreev's *Abyss*, and said :

"With regard to Leonid Andreev, I always remember a story by Ginzburg about a boy who cannot pronounce the letter 'r' and says to his friend: 'I went for a walk and suddenly I see a wolf. . . . Are you fwightened? Are you fwightened?'

"So Andreev also keeps on asking me: 'Are you fwightened?' and I am not in the least frightened."

Yesterday the conversation was about the Hertzen, Bakunin, and Belinsky circle. Tolstoi said:

"The most characteristic thing about that circle was a kind of epicureanism, or at least the denial of, the complete failure to understand, a religious conception of the world. Doctor Nikitin, for instance, was surprised that I did not think Gogol mad. They thought him mad, because he believed in God. And they could not even understand what was going on in his soul."

Tolstoi spoke very disapprovingly of Belinsky's famous letter to Gogol.

Doctor Butkevich asked Tolstoi if he had read Maeterlinck's new play, *Monna Vanna*.

Tolstoi replied:

"Why should I? Have I committed a crime?"

Some one observed that common people are very seldom interested by *Power of Darkness*.

Tolstoi said :

" To interest the people one must write more simply and much more shortly, as Sophie Andreevna paints ; everything in profile and everything on the plane, and yet no other pictures are enjoyed so much by children. In the same way, form must be simple and primitive if it is to be enjoyed by the people."

Tolstoi went on to say :

" I have been thinking a great deal about it lately. There are two kinds of art, and both are equally needed—one simply gives pleasure and comfort to people, the other teaches them."

Yesterday Tolstoi criticized the scientists (he mentioned Mechnikov) for their denial and mis-understanding of a religious conception of the world.

Some one mentioned the new Russian University in Paris.

Tolstoi is sceptical about it and said :

" Some seventy young women come and listen to the professors who teach them."

Mme. Stakhovich said something about the harm that is done to the girl students, but Tolstoi said :

" Well, they are bad enough already without that."

July 28*th*. The other day we walked in the woods. Tolstoi sat down on his camp stool, which was given him by N. He sighed and said :

" Yes, poor fellow ! "

Then he turned to Marie Lvovna and asked :

" Masha, who's the poor fellow ? "

" I do not know, papa."

" Buddha. N. bespattered Socrates, and now he is going to do the same to Buddha."

Yesterday Tolstoi was showing us a portrait group of the Tolstoi brothers, and, pointing to his brother Nicolay, said :

" He was my beloved brother. He was the man of whom Turgenev justly said that he had not a single one of the faults which one must have in order to be a writer. And I, although it is wrong of me, must say of my son Leo, that he, on the contrary, has all these faults, but none of the gifts, which are needed for a writer."

Ilya Lvovich said to Mme. Stakhovich that a writer must himself experience everything in order to tell it to others.

Tolstoi replied :

" Mere technique is sometimes enough to describe what he has experienced. A real writer, as Goethe justly observed, must be able to describe everything. And I must say that, although I am not very fond of Goethe, he could do it."

To-day Tolstoi was enthusiastic about Mozart's operas, particularly about *Don Juan*. Together with the extraordinary richness of its melody, he rates very high its power to give in music the reflection of characters and situations. Tolstoi recalled the statue of the commander, the village scene, and especially the duel.

He said :

" I hear there a presentiment, as it were, of the tragic *dénouement*, together with the excitement and even the romance of the duel." . . .

Then Tolstoi turned the conversation to the importance and province of form in art :

" I think that every great artist necessarily creates his own form also. If the content of works of art can be infinitely varied, so also can their form. Once Turgenev and I came back from the theatre in Paris and discussed this. He completely agreed with me. We recalled all that is best in Russian literature and it seemed. that in these works the form was perfectly original. Omitting Pushkin, let us take Gogol's *Dead Souls*. What is it ? Neither a novel nor a story. It is a something perfectly original. Then there is the *Memoirs of a Sportsman*, the best book Turgenev ever wrote ; then Dostoevsky's *House of the Dead*, and then, sinner that I am, my *Childhood*; Hertzen's *Past and Thoughts*; Lermontov's *Hero of our Time*. . . ."

August 1st. Tolstoi talked with Marie Alexandrovna Schmidt in my presence about a certain Khokhlov who went mad.

Tolstoi told me his story briefly, and then said:
" What a riddle insanity is! What is he—alive or dead? "

I said that insanity is not a greater riddle than sanity. The mystery is how the personality which lives in me manifests itself through the brain. But if I admit that the first cause is not in my brain, but outside it, and the brain is only a means by which my personality is shown, then it is for me no *fresh* mystery that that personality of mine cannot be manifested when the machine of the brain is disordered.

Tolstoi said:
" Yes, it is all a mystery! Let us take a child. When it is born, has it conscious life? When does consciousness begin in a child? And what is it when it moves in its mother's womb? To me life is a ceaseless liberation of the ' I ' of the spirit. Recently N. N. came to me and asked me whether I believe in a future life? But to me there is a contra-

diction contained in the question. What does 'future life' mean? One may believe in life, but for eternal life our conception 'future' is quite inapplicable.

"But if we speak of life as we can realize it, as life *after* our present life, then it seems to me that it can be conceived only in two possible forms: either as a fusion with the eternal spiritual principle, with God, or as a continuation, in a different form, of the same process of liberation of the spiritual 'I' from what is called matter.

"It may be accidental, but it is remarkable that Christ said to the Pharisees: 'Before Abraham was, I am.'"

I came into the dining-room while Tolstoi was talking with K. A. Mikhailov about art:

"Among the sensations experienced by our senses of touch, sight, hearing, etc., there are some which are unpleasant and painful—for instance, a violent knock, a deafening noise, a bitter taste, etc. Now modern art often works upon us not so much by means of its content, as by irritating our organs of sensation, painfully. As regards taste, an unhealthy taste needs mustard, whilst it produces an unpleasant impression upon a pure taste. So it is in the arts. It is necessary to draw a dividing line and to find

where that artistic mustard begins, and I think
it is a problem of enormous importance. In
painting, it seems to me, it is particularly difficult
to draw that line."

Tolstoi said to Count Yashvil :
" I have been learning all my life and do not
cease to learn, and this is what I have noticed :
learning is only fruitful when it corresponds to
one's needs. Otherwise it is useless. I remember I was a Justice of the Peace ; I used
to take the laws and tried to study them, but I
could not fix anything in my mind. But whenever for some particular case, I needed certain
legal knowledge, I always kept it in my mind
and could use it in practice."
The conversation turned on our government.
Count Yashvil began giving instances to prove
how bad it is in Europe.
To this Tolstoi replied even with some
irritation :
" What right have we to condemn anything
in the West, when we are still so far behind
them ? Our government is so abominable that
we have no right at all to condemn any one.
We are without the possibility of satisfying the
most elementary needs of every man : to read,
write, think what and how one wishes."

Tolstoi was now writing *Hadji-Murat*, and he said :

" I remember how a long time ago some one gave me a travelling candlestick for a present. When I showed the candlestick to our Yasnaya Polyana carpenter, he looked at it, looked again, and then sighed and said : ' It is crude stuff ! ' The same applies to my present work : it is crude stuff ! "

Yasnaya Polyana, August 30th. I have been here now for three days. Tolstoi talked with Ilya Lvovich and some one else about farming and about the new machine called " The Planet."

Tolstoi said :

" It is surprising how few technical inventions and improvements have been made in agriculture, compared with what has been done in industry."

Afterwards Tolstoi said :

" Ruskin says how much more valuable human lives are than any improvements and mechanical progress."

Then Tolstoi added :

" It is difficult to argue with Ruskin : he by himself has more understanding than the whole House of Commons."

Tolstoi went for a walk, and I fetched him his

overcoat. I met him on the road. We walked home together and walked through the fields.

Tolstoi looked at the bad harvest and said :

" My farmer's eye is exasperated : God alone knows how they sowed ! "

When we reached the boundary of the Yasnaya Polyana forest, we heard the loud voices of children, and soon we saw a motley crowd of village boys discussing something. They noticed Tolstoi and began urging one another to go up to him—then they felt shy and hid themselves. Tolstoi became interested in them and beckoned to them. They began to approach, at first timidly and one by one, but gradually all came together. I particularly remember one of them dressed in grey calico striped trousers, in a ragged cap and shirt, with huge heavy boots, probably belonging to his father.

Tolstoi showed them his camp stool, which was a great success. He asked them what they were doing there. It appeared they had been picking pears and the watchman ran after them. Tolstoi walked with them. On the way he enquired about their parents. One boy turned out to be the son of Taras Fokanich.

Tolstoi said to me :

" He was one of my very best pupils. What a happy time that was ! How I loved that work! And, above all, there was nobody in my way. Now my fame is always in my way : whatever I do, it is all talked about. But at that time nobody knew or interfered, neither strangers nor my family—though, there was no family then."

When we reached the spot Tolstoi told the children to gather the pears. They climbed the trees, some knocking down the pears, others shaking them down, others again picking them up. There was a hubbub, a happy noise of children; and the figure of the good old Tolstoi lovingly protecting the children from the attack of the watchman moved one to tears. Then two or three peasants came to ask his advice on some legal point.

Tolstoi, Nikitin, and I talked of Dostoevsky.

Tolstoi said :

" Certain characters of his are, if you like, decadent, but how significant it all is ! "

Tolstoi mentioned Kirilov in *The Possessed*, and said :

" Dostoevsky was seeking for a belief, and, when he described profoundly sceptical characters, he described his own unbelief."

Of Dostoevsky's attitude to " Liberalism " Tolstoi observed :

" Dostoevsky, who suffered in person from the Government, was revolted by the banality of Liberalism."

Tolstoi said :

" During the sixty years of my conscious life a great change has come over us in Russia—I am speaking of the so-called educated society— with regard to religious questions : religious convictions were differentiated; it is a bad word, but I don't know how to express it differently. In my youth there were three, or rather four, categories into which society in this respect could be divided. The first was a very small group of very religious people, who had been freemasons previously, or sometimes monks. The second, about 70 per cent of the whole, consisted of people who from habit observed church rituals, but in their souls were perfectly indifferent to religious problems. The third group consisted of unbelievers who observed the conventions in cases of necessity; and, finally, there were the Voltairians, unbelievers who openly and courageously expressed their un- belief. The latter were few in number—about 2 or 3 per cent. Now one has no idea whom one is going to meet. One finds the most contrary convictions existing side by side. Re- cently there have appeared the latest decadents of orthodoxy, the orthodox churchmen like Merezhkovsky and Rosanov.

"Many people were attracted to orthodoxy through Khomyakov's definition of the Orthodox Church, as a congregation of people united by love. What could be better than that? But the point is that it is merely the arbitrary substitution of one conception for another. Why is the Orthodox Church such a congregation of love-united people? It is the contrary rather."

1903

March 21*st*. Last week I went for a day to Yasnaya Polyana. I found Tolstoi well and cheerful.

Tolstoi is always much interested in the question of man's spiritual state during sleep.

He told me this time :

" In a dream one cries, or is happy or excited, and, when one wakes up and remembers the dream, one does not understand what made one cry or be happy or excited. I explain it to myself in this way : Apart from the happiness, excitement, or bitterness which are caused by definite events, there are also states of happiness, excitement, ecstasy, and grief. In such states an insignificant event is often sufficient to throw us into ecstasy, excitement, etc. In a dream, when one's consciousness does not act so consistently and logically, this state is expressed by the corresponding sensation which has often no external cause. For instance, in a dream one often feels utterly ashamed, and when one wakes up and sees that one's trousers are quietly hanging over a chair, one feels an extraordinary joy. That is why I so much love ' Popov's Dream.' [1] It gives a wonderful account of that sensation of shame in a dream, and, besides, all the characters are magnificently described. In spite of its comic nature, it is a real work of art."

June 1st. I returned from Yasnaya Polyana, where I spent a day. Tolstoi is planning a work of a philosophical nature, which he is greatly excited about at present. Speaking of it, Tolstoi said to me :

" Everything in the world is alive. Everything that seems to us dead seems so only because it is either too large or, on the contrary, too small. We do not see microbes, and heavenly bodies seem dead to us, for the same reason that we seem dead to an ant. The earth is undoubtedly alive, and a stone on the earth is the same as a nail on a finger. The materialists make matter the basis of life. All these theories of the origin of species, of protoplasm, of atoms, are all of value in so far as they help us to know the laws governing the visible world. But it must not be forgotten that all these, including

[1] A comic poem by Count Alexey K. Tolstoi.

ether, are working hypotheses, and nothing else. Astronomers in their calculations assume that the earth is a motionless body, and only afterwards correct the mistake. Materialists too make false premises, but they do not observe the fact that this is so, but let them pass as basic truths.

" True life exists where the living being is conscious of itself as an indivisible ' I,' in whom all impressions, feelings, etc., become one. So long as the ' I ' struggles, as nearly the whole animal world does, merely to crush the other creatures known to him, in order to attain his own temporary advantage, true spiritual life which is without time and space remains unexpressed and imprisoned. True spiritual life is liberated when a man neither rejoices in his own happiness, nor suffers from his own suffering, but suffers and rejoices with the worries and pleasures of others and is fused with them into a common life.

" Of the life to come, although of course the words ' to come ' are inappropriate here, of life beyond our physical being, it is impossible to have knowledge. We can imagine two forms only : either a new form of the individual life, or a fusion of personal life in the life of the whole. The former seems to us more comprehensible and more likely, since we only know our individual life and we can more easily accept the idea of the same life in a different form."

July 14th. In the beginning of July my wife and I spent two days in Yasnaya Polyana.

On the occasion of Mme. Kolokoltsev's [1] suicide Tolstoi said to me : " I can't understand why people look upon suicide as a crime. It seems to me to be man's right. It gives a man the chance of dying when he no longer wishes to live. The Stoics thought like that."

As Mme. Kolokoltsev was insane, the conversation turned on insanity. I said, as I had done previously, that the spiritual life of the so-called insane remains unchanged. All that happens is that a mad person cannot make his personality felt. Tolstoi agreed with me.

Next day he said to me :

" Yesterday's conversation on insanity was of great interest to me. I have been thinking a great deal about it. There are two conscious-

[1] Mme. Kolokoltsev was the wife of the landowner N. A. Kolokoltsev. She suffered from nervous disorder and made several attempts at suicide. In spite of constant observation, she managed one night to make the blanket on the bed into a figure, and thus deceived her husband. She went into his study, opened the drawer of his table with a skeleton key, took out his revolver and shot herself. She was an elderly woman, the mother of two grown-up daughters.

nesses in us : one—the animal ; the other—the spiritual. The spiritual is not always shown in us, but it is this that makes our true spiritual life, which is not subject to time. I do not know how it is with you who are comparatively young, but with me there are times in my long life which are clearly preserved in my memory, and other times which have completely disappeared, they no longer exist. The moments which remain are most frequently the moments when the spirit in me awoke. It often happens at a time when one has done something wrong, and suddenly one wakes up, realizes that it is bad, and feels the spirit in one with special force. Spiritual life is a recollection. A recollection is not the past, it is always the present. It is our spirit, which shows itself more or less clearly, that contains the progress of man's temporary existence. There can be no progress for the spirit, for it is not in time. What the life in time is for, we do not know ; it is only a transitory phenomenon. Speaking metaphorically, I see this manifestation of the spirit in us as the breathing of God.

" There is a beautiful story about the unreality of time in *The Arabian Nights*. Some one was put into a bath ; he dipped his head in the water and saw a long history with most complicated adventures ; and then when he raised his head from the water, it turned out that he had only dipped his head in once ! "

Tolstoi was talking about Fedorov and Peterson, particularly about Fedorov :
" They belonged to the sect which believes in the resurrection of the dead here on earth. Their idea is that people must try to resurrect all those who have died in the past. They believe that by hard work for centuries mankind will achieve it. For this purpose one must study all things of antiquity and restore them. Fedorov was librarian to the Rumyantsev Museum and was a passionate collector of all old things : portraits, objects, etc. Mankind must cease to multiply and everything will be resurrected. That is their ideal. It turns out that Vladimir Solovev and Dostoevsky to some extent—there is a letter to this effect—believed in this idea.
" Fedorov, I think, is still alive. He must be over eighty. All his life he has lived as an ascetic. When I once visited him in the spring and saw his thin overcoat, I asked him : ' Do you wear a thin overcoat already ? ' and he replied : ' Christ said, if you have two cloaks, give them to him who has none, and I have two overcoats.' And after that he always wore only

a thin coat. He received a very small salary, ate very, very little, slept almost on the bare boards, helped the poor, and denied himself everything. He wrote a great deal, but his works remain in manuscript : his disciples have no money to publish them, and no publisher can be found to publish them."

There was a plague of poisonous flies at Yasnaya Polyana this summer which made one's face swell when they bit one.

Tolstoi said :

" Once, when I was younger, I wanted to write a story about a young man who stayed in the summer at a friend's house where there was a young girl. The very first day they fell in love and raved about each other. At night, when he was asleep, a fly bit his lip, and half his face swelled up. His lip and cheek were swollen, and his face looked idiotic. When the girl saw him in the morning their love at once came to an end. There were no more illusions : she noticed a number of faults in him which she had not noticed at all the day before."

The conversation was about Father Gregory Petrov.[1]

[1] G. S. Petrov, a publicist and politician who started his career as a preacher of the Church and then resigned his priesthood.

Tolstoi said of him :

" As was the case with Ambrosii of the Optino Monastery, he is becoming the slave of his popularity. Generally speaking, fame, popularity, is a dangerous thing. It is also harmful because it prevents one from looking upon people simply, in a Christian way. Now, for instance, I find Gorky very pleasant as a man, and yet I can't behave to him with perfect sincerity. His popularity prevents me from doing so. It is as if he were not in his right place. To him, too, his popularity is dangerous. His long novels are worse than his short stories, his plays are worse than his novels, and his addresses to the public are simply revolting.

" Yet as some one said : if my work is abused by every one, it means that there is something in it. If all praise it, it means that it is bad ; but if some praise it very much, and others dislike it very much, then it is first-rate. According to this theory Gorky's works are first-rate. Well, it may be so." . . .

A blind man came to Tolstoi, and Tolstoi was very much interested in him. The blind man was trying to get into a school for the blind, so as to complete his education, and Tolstoi wanted to help him. The blind man intended to give an account of his life. After lunch we were going for a walk. Tolstoi was talking to the blind man. Then he took him to the kitchen to give him some food, and said good-bye to him.

The blind man said to him :

" I should like to go on talking to you."

Tolstoi replied :

" Later, perhaps, I will talk to you again."

We went for a walk. But before reaching the gate Tolstoi said that he had changed his mind and would return home.

Sophie Andreevna observed :

" He probably regrets having left the blind man."

And it was true. We walked for a long time, and when we got back Tolstoi was still sitting with the blind man.

Tolstoi said to me later :

" The blind man told me many legends. One of them I never heard before :

" ' Once upon a time Christ and Peter the Apostle walked in the country and saw an old peasant making a fence out of reeds. Christ asked him : " Why, father, are you making such a weak fence of reeds ? " and the peasant replied : " I am old, it will last my lifetime." After that God saw to it that people should not know their age.' He also told me another legend, which I had heard before but in a different version :

" ' A just old man once lived in the woods. And people came to him and said : " Why do you never go to church ? " The old man listened to them and went with them. But while they took a boat to cross the river, the old man walked upon the water. They arrived and went into the church, but inside the church the devils stretched a skin on the floor and wrote down the names of the sinners on it. The old man looked and looked at this, then called the devils bad names, and they wrote his name down. On returning home he was unable to walk upon the water, but had to take the boat.' "

Tolstoi said :

" It is time for me to die, and I have a whole mass of subjects, and even a new one to-day. I have a whole long list of them." . . .

Tolstoi is going to expound in an artistic form Buddha's teaching, " Ta Twam Asi," the meaning of which is that in every man and his actions one can always recognize oneself.

Tolstoi recalled the following :

" When I was taken for the first time to a box in the Grand Theatre as a young child I saw nothing : I did not know that it was necessary to look at the stage sideways, and I looked straight in front of me at the opposite boxes."

August 12*th*. I spent the 7th and 8th in Yasnaya Polyana.

M. S. Sukhotin was talking about Count Bludov. Tolstoi said :

" His was a very interesting house where authors and the most interesting men of their time used to meet. I remember that I read there for the first time my *Two Hussars*. Bludov was once intimate with the Decembrists and sympathized in his soul with every progressive movement. And he kept on serving under Nicolas I."

Mikhail Sergeevich Sukhotin asked whether Bludov was a Russian, and why was he a Count ?

Tolstoi said :

" The Bludovs were a purely Russian family, to whom the title of Count was granted. I remember, when I gathered the peasants to read to them the Ukase of their liberation, at the bottom were the names of the signatories and it finished with the words : Countersigned by Count Bludov. An elderly peasant, Eremey, shook his head all the while and said : ' That Blud, he must be a brainy fellow ! ' Evidently he took it to mean that Bludov was at the head of the whole affair."

The conversation was about medicine. Tolstoi said :

" Medicine cannot possibly be called an ' experimental ' science, for in medicine experiment in the strict sense is impossible. With experiments in chemistry a repetition of the more or less same conditions is possible, and so there can be approximately an exact conclusion as to the results. But in medicine there is no exact experiment nor can there be, for it is never possible to repeat the conditions that existed previously ; if only because the individuality of the patient changes, and nearly, if not quite, everything changes in sympathy with that."

Tolstoi related this episode from his childhood :

" We had a distant relation—an old woman Yakovlev. She lived in her own house in the Staro-Konyushenna Street in Moscow. She was a great miser, and, when she went to the country in the summer, she sent her children ahead in the luggage van. Once, when I was quite a small child, old Yakovlev came to pay us a visit. She sat with the grown-up people, and my brother Nikolenka got a box, put dolls into it, and began dragging it across the rooms. When he dragged it into the room where old

Yakovlev sat, she asked him : 'Nicolas, what have you got there?' and he replied, 'It is old Yakovlev going into the country, and her children are being sent ahead in the luggage van.' " . . .

During the two days (the 6th and 7th August) of my stay in Yasnaya, Tolstoi wrote a perfectly new and very powerful story called *Father and Daughter*,[1] which, he said, "will stay as it is for the time being." Tolstoi himself seems to be very well pleased with the story, and he thinks he may not have to alter it.

Tolstoi recalled the folk-story of "Vanka Kliushnik," who asked before his execution to be allowed to sing a song ; and Tolstoi was in raptures over the beauty of it.

Tolstoi is much amused because he is riding a young horse and training it. He is a great connoisseur of horses ; he loves them and is a perfect horseman. He trains his horse to various paces. He showed me and Ilya Vasilevich how the horse started to gallop with the right leg. At the beginning of the ride I asked Tolstoi how to train a horse to start with this or that leg. Tolstoi explained to me how it was done, and then observed :

[1] Called in its final version, *After the Ball*.

" Once a horse leads off with a certain leg, it wants to start with the same leg next time. In a man's life, too, custom plays an enormous part. Once a certain habit is formed, a man unconsciously tries to act in accordance with it. It is very seldom that people act in accordance with reason, and only very remarkable people do so ; usually people live and act by habit. How otherwise could it be possible that moral truths, announced so long ago by the great thinkers and admitted by most people, so rarely guide their actions ? Very few people overcome the habits of animal life and oppose them by the convictions of reason."

When later we drove past a beautiful wood Tolstoi said :

" Once upon a time this forest belonged to Dolin-Ivansky. He was about to sell it and I wanted to buy it, but for some reason I bargained, although the price was reasonable. We did not settle the business. When I came home and thought it over, I saw that the price was reasonable and the forest good, and I sent the steward to say that I was ready to buy it. But when the steward arrived, the forest was already sold. For a long time afterwards I could not remember without annoyance that I had let that forest slip through my hands."

Then we drove by the forest called "Limonov Woods." It is a young forest planted by Tolstoi. He had not been there for a long time and was surprised to see how everything had flourished and grown up.

Tolstoi said :

" Yes, it is a queer sense, that of ownership : here, too, one finds the same habit. When one analyses it in one's own mind, the feeling disappears ; but instinctively one always sees in oneself a particular interest in what was or is one's property, although one considers ownership harmful and unnecessary."

Speaking later of the present political events Tolstoi said :

" The same is true also with regard to patriotism : unconsciously one's sympathies are on the side of Russia and her fortunes, and one catches oneself at it. But it is clear that with these internal and foreign troubles one fine day all of a sudden Russia may fall to pieces. As the saying goes : *sic transit gloria mundi*. Now it is an enormous and powerful state, and suddenly everything may go to pieces ! "

Tolstoi drew my attention to the fact that the road was beautifully lit up by the rays of the sun coming through the branches of the trees. He recalled that Turgenev in *Virgin Soil* has

described how Sipyagin met Mariana and Nezh-
danov lit up by such rays. He asked me if I
remembered the passage. I did not remember
it and said :
   " How do you remember it, Tolstoi ? "
   Tolstoi laughed and said :
   " But you remember in your music, and so we
writers remember things in our art."
   Tolstoi said about *Virgin Soil* that he did not
share the general indifference towards that novel
and considered it very successful. Among other
things, he thought the new type of Sipyagin
successful and observed at the right time.
   On this occasion Tolstoi said :
   " But for the most part I object to the trick
of guessing at modern types and phenomena.
The other day the painter K. was here. I told
him a great deal about his work which must be
unpleasant to him. He is always occupied with
these modern themes. I said to him that one
ought never to paint what is talked about in
the newspapers. Besides, he simply can't make
a picture intelligible, clear. In his works you
can't make out what he wants to represent.
How inferior he is to Orlov [1] in this respect ! "

   [1] N. V. Orlov, a painter from the people, of whose pictures
Tolstoi was very fond. Reproductions of most of his paintings hang
in Tolstoi's room.

I. V. Denisenko read aloud the chapters about Nicolas from *Hadji-Murat*.

Tolstoi sat in his room, but he wanted to come where we were all sitting.

He came in several times and said :

" It is not interesting ; let it be ! "

At last he even said with irritation :

" It is rubbish ! "

Then M. S. Sukhotin asked him :

" Why did you write it, then, Leo Nickolaevich ? "

Tolstoi replied :

" But it is not finished yet. You came into my kitchen, and no wonder it stinks with the smell of cooking."

Tolstoi explained why he had made up his mind never to write to the papers to deny what was said about him.

" When I stayed with Turgenev in Petersburg, Mefodii Katkov [1] arrived from Moscow, and, on behalf of his brother, asked Turgenev and myself to let him have something for his *Russkii Vestnik*. I promised nothing, but Turgenev with his characteristic kindness said, rather vaguely, that he might perhaps let him have something.

" Soon after this a group of writers in Petersburg, Nekrasov, Turgenev, myself, Panaev,

[1] The brother of the well-known editor M. N. Katkov.

Druzhinin, Grigorovich, formed ourselves into a group and decided to publish only in the *Sovremennik*. When Katkov heard this, he accused Turgenev in print of breaking his promise. Then I wrote a letter to Katkov, and asked him to publish it, in which I, as a witness, refuted Katkov's statement and proved that Turgenev had not promised Katkov anything.

" At first Katkov did not publish the letter ; afterwards he published it, but in such a mutilated form that it quite changed its character. After that I made a vow to myself that I would never make any reply to attacks in the Press."

The talk turned on our Government.

Tolstoi said :

" Do you know, Peter Alexeevich, I want to found a society whose members would bind themselves not to abuse the Government."

Sergeenko and others replied that, although it was true that people made too much of that subject, still, when the Government prevented people from living freely or breathing freely, it was difficult not to criticize it.

To this Tolstoi said :

" It is only necessary to remember that the Government, however strong and cruel it may be, can never prevent the real, spiritual life of man, which alone is of importance. And why wonder that the Government is cruel and wicked? So it must be. Mosquitoes bite, worms devour leaves, pigs grout in manure—all this suits them and it is not worth while to be indignant about it. I remember many years ago—my sons are now tall, bearded men, but they were then children—I once came into the dining-room downstairs in the Khamovniki house and saw that a ray of the sun fell across the whole room through the windows and made a bright spot on the sideboard which stood by the wall opposite the window. The ventilator was not tight shut and was moved by the wind, and as it moved the bright spot slid over the sideboard. I went in, showed the children the bright spot, and cried out: ' Catch it ! ' They all threw themselves on to the bright spot to catch it, but it raced, and it was difficult to catch it. But if one of the children succeeded in putting his hand on it, the bright spot showed on the top of his hand. That is like the spiritual nature of man : however you hide it, however much you try to suppress it or extinguish it, it will always remain the same and unchanged."

About writing Tolstoi said :

" If you ask some one : ' Can you play the violin ? ' and he says : ' I don't know, I have not tried, perhaps I can,' you laugh at him.

Whereas about writing, people always say : ' I don't know, I have not tried,' as though one had only to try and one would become a writer."

Tolstoi said about Jews :
" There are three kinds of Jews. Some are believers, religious, respecting their religion and strictly following its teaching. Others are cosmopolitan, standing on the highest step of consciousness ; and finally a third kind, the middle kind, almost the biggest class, at any rate of educated Jews, are even ashamed of being Jews or hide the fact, and at the same time they are hostile to other races ; but it is as if they hid their hostility behind the skirts of their overcoats. As my sympathies are with the first two classes, so the third is unsympathetic to me.

The conversation was about religion. Tolstoi said :
" Rousseau expressed a perfectly true idea that the Jewish religion admitted one revelation —the past ; the Christian religion two—the past and present ; and the Muhammadan three—the past, the present, and the future. Historically it is undoubtedly a progressive movement. Christianity is higher than Judaism, which is no longer alive. It is all in the past ; and

Muhammadanism is higher than Christianity : it has not the superstitions, the idolatry. To me personally Christianity, to be sure, is above all religions, but I speak about Christianity, not as the highest religious moral teaching, but as a historical fact. And as there is ever much in common between the opposite poles, so there is here ; both Judaism and Muhammadanism keep strictly to monotheism, and there is no intoxication in either ; but in the historical Christianity of the churches there is polytheism, as well as all kinds of ignorance and cruelty. Everything is justified and even encouraged."

1904

At Christmas Alexandra Lvovna made a Christmas tree in the lodge to entertain the village children. I do not know who made the choice, but, as there was not enough room, all the children were not admitted. Tolstoi, myself, and some one else, I don't remember who, came in rather later when the entertainment was at its height. At the door of the lodge stood the children who could not be admitted. When they saw us, the mothers of the children began asking Tolstoi to take their children with him. Tolstoi took two or three inside with him. It was bright and hot. Inside the burning candles flamed. It smelt of burnt branches. We soon came out.

Tolstoi said with a sigh :

" How wrong it is ! Some are inside and the others are not allowed in. When our children were small, Sophie Andreevna always had a Christmas tree, and the village children came to it. Once they gave us the scarlet fever, and after that they were no longer admitted, except a few who were carefully chosen. I remember once there was a Christmas tree upstairs. I was lying downstairs on the sofa (where the library now is), and I was terribly ashamed to think of the children crowding outside and not being let in. I remember I could not endure it, came out, and gave them three roubles, and of course made things still worse—they began to dispute and quarrel over the division of it, and it was revolting, shameful, and painful ! "

June 5th. Yasnaya Polyana.

On the day of our arrival, May 27th, Tolstoi talked at dinner about the Decembrists whom he knew after their return from banishment (he is again studying that period).

He spoke of Prince Volkonsky : [1]

" His appearance with his long grey hair was altogether like that of an Old Testament prophet. What a pity I spoke so little to him then, when I need him so much now ! He was a wonderful old man, the flower of the Petersburg aristocracy both by birth and by his position at Court. And then in Siberia, after he had already served hard labour, and his wife had something like a

[1] Prince S. G. Volkonsky (1788–1865), one of the most famous Decembrists, and his wife, *née* Raevsky (1805–1863). Both left remarkable memoirs.

136

salon, he worked with the peasants ; all sorts of tools for peasants' work were in his room."

Tolstoi does not believe the story about the affair between Poggio and Princess Volkonsky.

He said :

" I do not want to believe it : such scandals are so often invented and people's memory spoilt. Moreover, Poggio loved Volkonsky so much that when later (Volkonsky's wife being already dead) he felt the approach of death himself, he came to Volkonsky to die there."

Tolstoi went on to say :

" I made Volkonsky's acquaintance in Florence at Dolgorukov's, Koko Dolgorukov, the doctor. At that time it was rare for an aristocrat to become a doctor. It was when Nicolas I. limited the number of university students to three hundred, and Dolgorukov could not be admitted to any other faculty. He was a wonderfully capable man : he wrote poems, was a superb musician, painted pictures. He was married to (?). When I visited them for the first time in Florence, this was the scene I found : his wife and the well-known Marquis de Rogan were playing an extraordinary game : they made a mark on the wall and tried, by lifting their feet, to touch the mark ; each tried to lift his or her leg higher and higher.

" There was also present the very gifted painter Nikitin. He drew wonderfully in pencil. I remember he had an album and drew Volkonsky's portrait in it. He also drew mine. I wonder where the album is. If some collector were to get hold of it now ! "

Then at dinner Tolstoi told us two anecdotes from his life. The first was how he ate some earth-worms (Tolstoi told it because Alexandra Lvovna and Ilya Lvovich's children were going fishing). Tolstoi said he was carrying the worms in one hand, and a loaf of black bread in the other. He had finished eating the bread, and, thinking of something else, put the worms in his mouth and began chewing them, and for some time could not think what mess he had put in his mouth.

Tolstoi said :

" I remember the taste of them as if I were eating them now."

My wife asked him if it was very unpleasant.

" The taste of earth ; but I don't advise you to taste it."

Some one sneezed and Tolstoi told another story.

" I used to sneeze very loudly ; once at night I woke and felt I was going to sneeze immediately, and as Sophie Andreevna was going to have a baby, I was afraid to frighten her by sneezing. Half asleep I cried out : ' Sonia, I am going to sneeze ! ' Sophie Andreevna of course woke up and was frightened, and I instantly fell asleep without having sneezed."

Tolstoi also talked about Belogolovy's *Reminiscences*.[1] He seemed to Tolstoi a narrow-minded man. Speaking of the terrible impression made by his description of the diseases and deaths of Nekrasov, Turgenev, and Saltikov, Tolstoi said :

" How they dreaded death ! And then there were those horrible disgusting details of their illnesses, particularly Nekrasov's."

Last winter my wife and I stayed at Yasnaya Polyana, and, when we had to leave, Tolstoi was sitting in his room with P. A. Boulanger. We came into the room to say good-bye, and probably they were talking of Boulanger's family affairs.

We entered just as Tolstoi was saying :

" . . . if people only said more often : ' Do you remember ? ' People should make it a rule that if one person says or does something wrong in the heat of a quarrel, or when one is angry, the other should say : ' Do you remember ? ' "

---

[1] N. A. Belogolovy (1834–1895), doctor, author of the well-known *Reminiscences*, in which there is a chapter devoted to Tolstoi called " A Meeting with L. N. Tolstoi."

Tolstoi noticed my wife and me and said :

" Now, you young people, you ought to make that your rule ! No one can be such a friend as one's wife, a real friend. In marriage it is either paradise, or simple hell ; there is no ' purgatory.' "

Boulanger said that generally it was a case of purgatory.

Tolstoi thought for a time and then said with a sigh :

" Yes, perhaps, unfortunately." . . .

That same evening, looking at Andrey Lvovich's little girl, Sonechka, playing on the floor, Tolstoi said :

" Faust speaks of the rare moment of which one can say : ' Verweile doch, du bist so schön ! ' Now there it is, that moment ! " (Tolstoi pointed to the little girl.) " There is a perfectly happy, pure, and innocent moment."

June 20th. Some time ago, in May, Tolstoi said :

" Religions are usually based on one of these three principles : on sentiment, reason, or illusion. Stoicism is an example of the religion of reason ; Mormonism of illusion ; Muhammadanism of sentiment. I have lately received many letters from Muhammadans. I had a letter from Cairo from a representative of the Baptist sect, it is an example of the religion of sentiment. I also had a letter from India, written by a wonderful and very religious man. He writes that true Muhammadanism is a perfectly different thing from what people usually think it to be. Indeed, I know some very religious Moslems. And how movingly simple and lofty is their worship ! "

To-day at sunset we walked in the garden. We talked of Gorky and his feeble " Man." Tolstoi was saying that to-day on his walk he met on the road (he likes to go out on to the road, and sit down on a little stone, a milestone, and to observe or to speak to the passers-by) a man who turned out to be a rather well-educated working-man.

Tolstoi said :

" His outlook on the world agrees perfectly with Gorky's so-called Nietzscheism and the cult of the personality. It is evidently the spirit of the time. Nietzsche did not say anything new— his is now a very popular world-conception."

Then Tolstoi said :

" When I was a Justice of the Peace, there lived in Krapivna a merchant called Gurev, who used to say about young people of education : ' Well, I look at your students—they are all scholars, they know everything, only they have no invention.' Turgenev, I remember, liked this expression very much."

Recently a party of gypsies camped on the road near Yasnaya Polyana. Gypsies often roam about Yasnaya Polyana. The party usually stay for two or three days, and in the evenings the Yasnaya Polyana household comes out to hear the gypsy songs and enjoy their dances.

Tolstoi, looking at the gypsies, became a changed man, and involuntarily began to dance to their tunes, and to cry out again and again approvingly.

" What a wonderful people ! "

The old gypsies all know Tolstoi and always enter into conversation with him. Tolstoi from his youngest days loved and knew the gypsies and their peculiar life.

When we left the house, it was drizzling. Soon the rain got worse, and we returned.

Andrey Lvovich said :

" Now we have come to the house, the rain will stop."

And, indeed, on our way home the rain stopped, and we went back to the gypsies.

Tolstoi said :

" Yes, it is always like that : as soon as you

turn to go home the rain stops. Something like this happens in Moscow too. When you have to find some one in a large building and ring for the porter, he is never there. But no sooner do you go into the yard to make water than the porter is sure to catch you. So I advise you that if you have to find some one, don't ring for the porter, but do the second thing first."

When Andrey Lvovich was made an aide-de-camp, Tolstoi said to him :

" My only comfort is that you are sure not to kill a single Japanese. An aide-de-camp is always exposed to great danger, but seldom takes part in the fighting. I spent a great deal of time on the fourth bastion at Sevastopol when I was in the army on the Danube. I was aide-de-camp, and I believe I had not to fire even once. I remember once on the Danube, near Silistria, we were on our side of the river, but there was also a battery on the other side, and I was sent across with some order. The commander of the battery, Schube, on seeing me, thought: ' Well, there's that little Count, I'll give him a lesson ! ' And he took me across the whole line under fire, and with deadly slowness on purpose. I passed that test well outwardly, but my feelings were not pleasant. I also remember how one of the highest officers—Kotsebu—visited the bastion in Sevastopol, and some one, I think it was Novosilzev, wanted to put him to the test, and began saying perpetually : 'Look, Your Excellency, just there at their line,' forcing him to put his head out from behind the fortifications. He put his head out once or twice, and then, realizing what was up, he, as the superior officer, began in his turn to order the other man to look at the firing, and, after teasing him for some time, he said : 'Next time I advise you not to doubt the courage of your superiors.' "

Tolstoi recalled Lichtenberg's [1] aphorism to the effect that mankind will finally perish when not a single savage is left.

Tolstoi added :

" I first turned to the Japanese, but they have already successfully adopted all the bad sides of our culture. The Kaffirs are the only hope remaining."

Tolstoi said :

" I do not remember during any previous war such depression and anxiety as are now in Russia. I think it is a good sign, a proof that a realization of the evil and uselessness and absurdity of war is permeating deeper and deeper

[1] G. C. Lichtenberg (1742-1799), German physicist, critic, and publicist.

the social consciousness ; so that perhaps the time is coming when wars will be impossible— nobody will want to go to war. Now Lisanka, who always sees the good in things, was telling me about a peasant—a porter, I think—who was called up and, before going to the front, took off his cross. That is a truly Christian spirit! Although he is not able to resist the general will and has to yield to it, yet he clearly realizes that it is not God's doing."

Tolstoi described with horror how a priest marched with his cross in his hand in front of the soldiers.

June 26*th*. Last week I reached Yasnaya in the evening. The Sukhotins were there. During tea Misha Sukhotin began to tell Tolstoi that on completing his studies at the School of Juris- prudence he would like to go to Paris to continue his studies ; and he began to argue with Tolstoi. I did not hear the beginning of the argument. I came in when Tolstoi was saying :

" . . . Every man is a perfectly individual being, who has never existed before and will never happen again. It is just the individuality, the singularity of him, which is valuable ; but school tries to efface all this and to make man after its own pattern. The pupils of the Tula secondary school came to me lately and asked what they should do. I said to them: above all, try to forget everything you have been taught."

Tolstoi thinks the Russian University in Paris perfectly useless and good-for-nothing. He said:

" The best educational institution that I know is the Kensington Museum in London. There is a large public library where many people work, and they have professors of various special subjects. Every one who works, if he has a question to ask, gives notice of it, and, when several such questions have accumulated, the professor issues a notice to say that he will lecture on such and such subjects, and those who wish may come and hear him. Such an arrangement is most in keeping with the true object of teaching—to answer the questions which arise in the minds of the students. But in every other institution, lectures which are of no use to the student are read by professors who are for the most part entirely without gift. None of these lecturers would dare to publish their lectures. Goethe said:

" ' When I speak it turns out better than when I think; I write better than I speak; and what I publish is better than what I write.' He meant by this that what a man publishes is usually the cream of his thought, the thing he most believes in. Instead of going to Paris to attend lectures, go to the public library, and you won't come out for twenty years, if you really wish to learn. One ought not to talk about oneself, but I must say this : when I was at the University in Kazan I did practically nothing the first year. The second year I began to work. There was a Professor Mayer who took an interest in me and gave me, as a subject, to compare the code of Catherine the Great with Montesquieu's *Esprit des lois*. And, I remember, I became infatuated with the work. I went into the country and began to read Montesquieu ; this reading opened up endless horizons ; I began reading Rousseau, and left the University for the simple reason that I wanted to work; for at the University I should have to occupy myself with subjects that did not interest me and were of no use to me."

Sergey Lvovich asked Tolstoi why he did not go in for his examinations at Petersburg University.

Tolstoi said :

" I began to work hard, passed two examinations, was awarded two marks of distinction, but then it was spring ; it drew me to the

country; well, I gave it up and went away."
. . . Speaking of the good effects upon men of having received no education, Tolstoi said :
"I know two musicians who never went to school, and yet they are very well-educated men, who, whatever subject you talk about, know it thoroughly,—G. and Sergey Ivanovich Taneev.

I played.   Then Tolstoi said :
"Anton Rubinstein told me that, if he is moved himself by what he is playing, he ceases to move his audience.   This shows that the creation of a work of art is only possible when the emotion has settled in the artist's mind."
I do not remember how the conversation now got upon writing, but Tolstoi said :
"Usually when I begin a new book I am very pleased with it myself and work with great interest.   But as the book work goes on, I become more and more bored, and often in re-writing it I omit things, substitute others, not because the new idea is better, but because I get tired of the old.   Often I strike out what is vivid and replace it by something dull."
The conversation turned upon Hertzen.   Tolstoi read aloud extracts from his book (a collection of articles published in the *Kolokol*).   Tolstoi is extremely fond of Hertzen and values him very

highly. He spoke of Hertzen's unhappy private life and of the suffering he went through when the representatives (particularly the younger representatives) of the party with whom he had worked throughout his life deserted him and ceased to understand him.

Tolstoi saw Hertzen in London, when Hertzen lived with Mme. Tuchkov-Ogarev.

Biryukov asked Tolstoi (for the biography of Tolstoi which he is writing) about his conversation with Hertzen which Mme. Ogarev refers to in her *Reminiscences.*

Tolstoi said that he remembered a great many of their talks, but not that particular one. And he added :

" Perhaps she merely invented the conversation, as the authors of memoirs and reminiscences so often do."

On the whole, Tolstoi has not a high opinion of Mme. Ogarev, although he says he knows her but little.

He said :

" I received a letter from her in which she, as though to justify herself, gives an account of the affair with the peasants which had lately taken place on her estate. There were some fields there which the peasants had had the use of from time immemorial. The fields belonged legally to the landowner. A bailiff was engaged, a Pole called Stanislavski, and he drove the peasants' cattle from the fields on to the estate. The peasants collected with thick sticks in their hands to free their cattle, determined not to give up the use of the fields. They arrived at the Manor and began by demanding their cattle. Finally, Stanislavski fired, and killed or wounded, I do not remember which, some one in the crowd. The crowd became furious and threw themselves on Stanislavski, who tried to save himself by flight, but he was overtaken on a moor and was murdered in a most brutal way. As a result of the affair, a military court was held and two or three peasants were hanged."

Tolstoi had known of this before he got her letter, and was horrified at the incredible verdict.

Afterwards Tolstoi said :

" Lately I got a letter from a lady asking me why, strictly speaking, it is a crime to kill. Anyhow man must die sooner or later—is it not all the same? I replied that since every man represents a unique type, which never occurs again, we have and can have no absolute knowledge of why he is needed for the life of all. In life everything is very carefully arranged, and we do not know the reason why just this individual should be alive, and it is for this reason that the destruction of this unique creature appears so terrible."

Of being afraid in battle, Tolstoi said :

" It is impossible not to be afraid. Every one is afraid, but tries to conceal it. When wounded have to be carried off the battlefield, so many men volunteer for the work that the officers have to use great force to keep the soldiers back, since every one wants, even for a time, to get out of fire."

Of himself Tolstoi said that he was never so much afraid as upon the night before the attack on Silistria, which after all did not take place.

Then Tolstoi said :

" The Japanese are less afraid, for they evidently value life much less than Europeans do. The absence of the fear of death goes to extreme lengths with some people. For instance, if a Chukcha wants to spite his enemy, he comes to his hut and kills himself near it, knowing that his enemy will then have much trouble with legal proceedings.

July 8th. Tolstoi said with regard to his article about war, " Bethink Yourselves " :

" It is painful to feel that my words go unheeded. If one is dealing with the so-called men of science who regard war, apart from its moral significance, as one of the stages in the evolution of human relations, then, at any rate, one knows where one is. But what is one to do and how is one to speak to people who evidently cannot understand my point of view? Whatever I say glides off them. They are, as it were, greased with a sort of oil, so that everything runs off them, like water, without wetting them."

After this Tolstoi said that, when he wrote to Nicolas II. (from the Crimea, in the winter of 1901–1902), he was told that Nicolas II. " read his letter with pleasure." He also recollected Hertzen's letters to Alexander II.

Tolstoi wrote to Nicolas II. about the land question.

With reference to the attitude in Government circles to that question Tolstoi said :

" I can't possibly put myself at their point of view. I remember when I was young and an officer I was never bothered by these questions ; somehow they did not arise in me. But I cannot imagine that I should pass by such a problem, if I happened to come across it. I remember two such cases in my life. One, when Vasili Ivanovich Alexeev,[1] when I was at the height of my career as a landlord, expressed

[1] V. I. Alexeev, at that time tutor of Tolstoi's son Ilya.

to me for the first time the idea that the ownership of land is evil. I remember how much I
was struck by the idea, and how at once perfectly
new horizons opened before me. So it also
happened when some one, I don't remember
who it was, I think a Frenchman, told me that
prostitution was an abnormal thing, and not
only useless, but really harmful to mankind.
Schopenhauer, for instance, says that it is only
owing to prostitution that family relations are
still preserved in the community. I had not
previously thought about it, but, on hearing the
Frenchman speak, I at once felt the truth of what
he said and could no longer go back. I can
imagine that one's thoughts may not tend in a
certain direction ; one may be ignorant of some
point of view. But I cannot understand that
incapacity and unwillingness to learn."

July 9th. Speaking of Lichtenberg's aphorisms Tolstoi said :

" Aphorisms are perhaps the best way of
expounding philosophical judgments. For instance, Schopenhauer's aphorisms (*Parerga and
Paralipomena*) express his conception of the
world much more clearly than *The World as
Will and Imagination*. A philosopher, in ex-
plaining a whole complicated system, sometimes

involuntarily ceases to be honest. He becomes the slave of his system, for the symmetry of which he is often prepared to sacrifice the truth."

Speaking of Lichtenberg's beautiful German style, Tolstoi said :

" Every literary language reaches its highest point and then begins to decline. In the German language that time was at the end of the eighteenth and the first half of the nineteenth century ; it was the same with the French language. Now both in Germany and France the language has become utterly spoilt. In Russia we are now finding ourselves on the border-line. The Russian language has quite lately reached its apex and now it begins to decay."

Tolstoi praised Chekhov's language very highly for its simplicity, compactness, and expressiveness. Gorky's language he disapproves of, thinking it artificial and rhetorical.

When Nicolas II. appeared in many places to bless the troops going to the Japanese war with icons, Tolstoi said :

" If A, the ruler of a huge country, takes a board, B, in his hand and kisses it in the presence of crowds of many thousands of kneeling troops and then waves the board over the heads of those who stand in front of him, and does this all over the country, what except trash can come from such a country ? This has never happened before. In your own room you may do whatever you like. One man likes to wash himself with wine or eau-de-Cologne, another kisses icons if he likes, but such idolatry on a large scale in the face of all and such deception of the crowd are simply incredible ! " . . .

During the war Tolstoi always said that in spite of his attitude to war and to patriotism generally, he felt in the depth of his soul an instinctive sorrow at Russian defeats.

I heard him say this in the presence of G., B., and some others. All of them energetically denied in themselves any such instinctive " patriotic bias." It seems to me that they were simply afraid of admitting it even to themselves.

October 22nd. Mechnikov sent Tolstoi his book (*Studies on the Nature of Man*) in French. Tolstoi read it through.

To-day he said to me :

" I got much interesting information out of the book, for Mechnikov is undoubtedly a great scientist. But the self-satisfied narrowness with which he is convinced that he has solved almost all problems that agitate man is surprising in him. He is so sure that man's happiness consists in a state of animal contentment that he calls old age an evil (because of its limited capacity of physical enjoyment), and does not even understand that there are men who think and feel precisely the opposite. But I value my old age and would not exchange it for any earthly blessings."

The conversation turned on the tendency of women to crowd to universities.

Tolstoi said smilingly :

" If I were a Minister of Education, I should issue a Ukase by which all women were obliged to enter universities and would be deprived of the right to marry and have children. For the infringement of this law the guilty would be liable to a heavy fine. Then all of them would be sure to marry ! "

Tolstoi spoke on August 28th with exasperation about writing as a profession. I have rarely seen him so agitated :

He said :

" One ought only to write when one leaves a piece of one's flesh in the ink-pot each time one dips one's pen."

1905

January 5th. During the Christmas holidays Misha Sukhotin read Professor Korkunov's book on Russian State Law. Tolstoi took it and began to read it. He sat nearly the whole evening in his room, and came out in a state of agitation and disturbance saying : " It gave me palpitation of the heart to read that ! In this, as in almost all legal books which deal with ' rights ' of different kinds, it talks of anything and everything except the truth of the matter. It deals with the ' subject ' and ' object ' of right—I never could make out what precisely those words and others of the same sort mean, nor could I ever get any one to explain them to me. But whenever the argument approaches the real question, the author immediately swerves aside and hides himself behind his objects and subjects."

Further Tolstoi said :

" This is what surprises me ; all my life I have striven for knowledge. I sought and still seek for it, and the so-called men of science say that I denounce science. All my life I have been occupied with religious questions, and outside of them I see no sense in human life; yet the so-called religious men consider me an atheist." . . .

About that time, in January, Tolstoi said that he should like to write a whole series of stories for his " Reading Circle " which he is now planning, and that he had already many subjects in mind.

" Only one minute of life remains, and there's work for a hundred years," he said.

When later in the evening I played Chopin's prelude, Tolstoi said :

" Those are the kind of short stories one ought to write ! "

There was then an interesting talk about Chekhov's story, *The Darling*, with reference to Gorbunov's letter dissuading him from publishing the story in the "Reading Circle." Tolstoi on the contrary decided to include the story without fail, and expressed his very high opinion of it; and in a few days he wrote a preface to *The Darling* in which he expressed his feeling for it.

Of Gorbunov's letter Tolstoi said :

" I feel a woman's influence on him in this. The confused modern idea is that a woman's capacity to give herself up with all her being to love is obsolete and done with; and yet this is the most precious and the best thing in her and her true vocation; and not political meetings, scientific courses, revolutions, etc."

Of Beethoven's music Tolstoi said that at times he felt a little bored by it, as he thought often happens with what has once struck one greatly. He felt the same, for instance, about Ge's paintings.

June 16th. In February I made a note of Tolstoi's words :

" Immortality, incomplete, of course, is certainly realized in our children. How strongly man desires immortality, is most clearly shown by his endeavour to leave some trace after his death. It might seem of no importance to a man what is said of him and whether he is remembered after he has gone; and yet what efforts he makes for it ! "

Tolstoi said of the Molokans that he had no sympathy with their religious formalism. In this respect he draws a parallel between the Molokans and the English.

The son of Vicomte de Vogüé visited Tolstoi in the spring ; Tolstoi said of him :

" He is a typical Frenchman in everything— from his trousers to his way of thought. His father translated *Three Deaths* and wrote to me about it long ago. It was on my conscience that I did not answer him, and was glad to have the opportunity of apologizing to his son."

Tolstoi was surprised by young de Vogüé's saying that his father worked at night and smoked a great deal during his work.

Tolstoi said :

" I imagine that a Frenchman must in the morning rub himself red with eau-de-Cologne, drink his coffee, and sit down quietly to work.

" I always write in the morning. I was pleased to hear lately that Rousseau too, after he got up in the morning, went for a short walk and sat down to work. In the morning one's head is particularly fresh. The best thoughts most often come in the morning after waking, while still in bed or during the walk. Many writers work at night. Dostoevsky always wrote at night. In a writer there must always be two people—the writer and the critic. And, if one works at night, with a cigarette in one's mouth, although the work of creation goes on briskly, the critic is for the most part in abeyance, and this is very dangerous."

Tolstoi often says that he cannot find a suitable definition of music.

Once in the spring he said :

" Music is the shorthand of emotion. Emotions which let themselves be described in words with such difficulty, are directly conveyed to man in music, and in that is its power and significance."

Once, a long time ago, Tolstoi said :

" Life is the present. All that a man has felt remains with him as a memory. We always live by memories. I often feel more strongly not what I have actually felt, but what I have written and felt in describing my characters. They too have become my memories, as if they had been actual experiences."

The other day the talk was on the same lines. Tolstoi said :

" A so-called misfortune happens ; one does not usually feel it, just as one does not feel a wound at the moment it is inflicted ; and it is only by degrees that the sorrow grows in strength, having become a memory, placed, that is, not outside me, but already within. Yet, after a long life, I notice that the bad and painful things have not become me ; they have somehow passed by ; but on the contrary, all the pleasant feelings, all the loving relations towards people—my childhood, all that has been good—rise with particular clearness in my memory."

Tatyana Lvovna said :

" But how do you explain Pushkin's poem ;

' Memory unfolding its long scroll,' and further :
' And reading my life with disgust, I tremble
and curse ' ? "

Tolstoi replied :

" That is quite different. To be able to
experience and feel all that is bad in one with such
power—that is a precious and necessary quality.
Happy and of great importance is the man who
can go through it with the vigour of Pushkin."

July 6th. We went for a walk to the sandpits.
During the walk Gorbunov asked Tolstoi about
Alexander Dobrolyubov's[1] religious and philo-
sophic book.   Tolstoi said of the book :

" It is vague, false, and artificial."

On that occasion the talk was about the
literary profession.

Tolstoi said :

" It is surprising how in even a little piece of
work one must think it over from all points of
view before starting it.   It does not matter
whether you are making a shirt or a move in
chess.   And if you do not think it out, you at
once spoil it all—you won't make the shirt,
you'll lose the game.   It is only in writing that

[1] A. M. Dobrolyubov (1876), religious seeker. His adherents
formed a " Dobrolyubovian sect " on the basis of Christian anarchy.
D. began his literary activity as a poet of the decadent school.

one can do what one likes, and people never notice—indeed one can become a famous writer."

Tolstoi went on to say :

" The whole business of the writer is to perfect himself. I have always tried and try now to make a question which interests me clear to the highest degree that I am capable of making it. The writer's work consists in that. The most dangerous thing is to be a teacher. I do not think I have tried to be that. Yes, I have. . . . But always badly."

I. Gorbunov was saying that the " Posrednik " had the Censor's permission to publish an excellent little book, in which a visit to Sarov is described impartially.

Tolstoi said :

" I have no sympathy when such things are described in a joking or jeering way. There is a great deal of sincere, simple belief there which should be treated carefully. In some old credulous woman you feel, in spite of the absurd superstition, that the foundation of her faith is a real striving for the highest and for the truth. Her outlook on the world is much higher than that of a professor who has solved all questions long ago."

V. G. Kristi who walked with us asked Tolstoi: " If such an old woman talked about religion, must one destroy her illusions and tell her honestly what one thinks ? "

Tolstoi replied to him :

" The question does not exist to me. If I talk about religious questions, I always express my thoughts, if I believe the truth of what I say; and if my words are not understood, it is none of my business, but I can say only what I think."

Last year two young men came to Tolstoi, and now they have been again. They are very nice and in search of a better life. They turned out to be ballet dancers from the Moscow Grand Theatre. The necessity of maintaining their family prevents them from changing their profession. Tolstoi praised them highly. Then with a smile he said :

" If I had children now, I should send them to the ballet. At any rate it is better than the university. Their feet alone might be spoilt in the ballet, but at the university it is their heads."

Tolstoi compared marriage to a little boat in which two people sail over a stormy ocean.

" Each must sit tight and not make sharp movements or the boat will upset."

Speaking of the present schemes for a constitution in Russia Tolstoi said :

" The misfortune is in that the Radicals and their set will only try to say something very clever, to play the part of Russian Bebels, and the party game will constitute the whole of the activity of the representatives of the people."

Of the war Tolstoi said :
" The comforting side of the Russian failure in the war consists in this, that, however much people distort the genuine Christian teaching, yet its meaning has already permeated the consciousness of the people so deeply that war cannot become to them, as to the Japanese, a sacred cause by sacrificing his life to which a man becomes a hero and does a great deed. The view of war, as an evil, permeates the consciousness of the people, deeper and deeper.

Tolstoi said about the Japanese :
" The Japanese are perfectly incomprehensible and unknown to me. I see their wonderful capacity for adapting and even for carrying further the superficial side of European culture, chiefly in its worse aspects, but the soul of the Japanese is absolutely dark to me. Japan, by the way, proved that the whole of the boasted European civilization of a thousand years could be taken over and even surpassed in a few decades."

The conversation was about crowd psychology.

Tolstoi said :

" It is an interesting and still little explored problem. It is a hypnotism which has a terrible power over men. There is one moment when it is still possible to resist it. I am now no longer infected by others' yawning, because I always remember it. When you see a crowd running, you have to remember that you do not know why they run, and to look back ; and immediately you have dissociated yourself from the crowd, you are at once saved from the danger of succumbing to the hypnotism."

We played chess on the terrace, and in the hall Sophie Nicolaevna sang Schubert's " Wanderer."

Tolstoi said :

" Ah that Schubert ! he did a lot of harm ! "

I asked how ?

" Because he had in a high degree the power of making music correspond to the poetry of the text. This rare power of his has brought to birth a great deal of music which pretends to correspond to poetry, and that is a revolting kind of art."

They sang Glinka. Tolstoi said :

" Now, sinful man . . ." The interesting state of the game prevented him from finishing his sentence.

Later he said :

" I feel that Glinka was coarse, a sensual man. One always feels the man himself in his music. The young Mozart—bright and direct; the simple Haydn; the stern, conceited Beethoven— are all heard in their music."

Tolstoi is writing an article which is called " The Beginning of the End."

There was a newspaper correspondent to whom Tolstoi expressed a few of the ideas which made the basis of his article.

" The present movement in Russia is a world movement, the importance of which is still little understood. This movement, like the French Revolution formerly, will perhaps give, by means of its ideas, an impetus for hundreds of years to come. The Russian people has in the highest degree the capacity for organization and self-government. They gave up their power to the Government and waited, as they formerly did for the liberation of the serfs, for the liberation of the land. They have not been given the land, and they themselves will carry out that great reform. Our revolutionaries are perfectly ignorant of the people and do not understand this movement. They might help it, but they only hamper it. In the Russian people, it seems to me, and I think I am not biased, there is more of the Christian spirit than in other peoples. Probably the reason is that the Russian people got to know the New Testament about five centuries before the people of Europe, who until the Reformation hardly knew it."

Tolstoi criticized the complexity and artificiality of modern art in general, and of music in particular. He said :

" Certainly, if I love art, I can't love *no* art, but I must love that which exists. Still I have always before me the ideal of the highest art : to be clear, simple, and accessible to all."

I was saying how long and systematically one must teach piano-playing in order to be able to play well. Tolstoi found that " system " dangerous.

He said :

" In doing this one may lose the direct fresh feeling with which you regard a new work of art. I know it from my own experience—when one begins to write something, one works with excitement and interest, and the work goes well ; but then the same old thing begins to tire one and it becomes boring. Of course, there is the love of one's work, and the love is stronger than the boredom, and by love the boredom is overcome, but still boredom there is."

I spoke about the complexity of certain of Chopin's works, whom Tolstoi loves very much.

"Well, he too makes mistakes," Tolstoi replied smilingly. "Once I stayed with the Olsufevs in the country, and, referring to the weather and the gathering in of the harvest, I said to the old butler there—he was a sceptic and pessimist—that God knows what He does, to which he replied: 'He too makes mistakes!'"

Of creative activity Tolstoi said:

"The worst thing of all is to begin a work with the details; then one gets muddled and loses the power of seeing the whole. One has to behave like Pokhitonov who has spectacles with double glasses divided in two (looking at the distance and at his work), to look now through these and now through those and to put on now the bright and now the dark glasses."

July 28*th*. Biryukov showed Marie Nikolaevna (Tolstoi's sister) some old letters written by her brother Nikolay in French. Tolstoi recalled then that from childhood he was so much used to writing French that he kept the habit until he was quite grown up. When he lived in Paris with Turgenev, he once sat down to write a letter to his brother. Turgenev came up and, seeing that he was writing in French, was surprised and asked Tolstoi why he did it. Tolstoi said that until that moment it seemed to him that it was impossible to do otherwise, so used was he to writing letters in French.

On account of Biryukov's visit (he is writing Tolstoi's biography) and the arrival of his sister Marie Nikolaevna, Tolstoi again turned to memories of the past. He said :

" It is surprising how all the past becomes *me*. It is in me, like something folded. But it is difficult to be perfectly sincere. Sometimes I remember the bad only, another time the opposite. Lately I have remembered only the bad acts and events. It is difficult in this to keep the balance, so as not to exaggerate one way or another."

Tolstoi said :

" It is impossible to know anything about God ; He is a necessary hypothesis or, more truly speaking, the only possible condition of a right moral life. As an astronomer must base his observations upon the earth as a motionless centre, so also man cannot live rightly and morally without the idea of God. Christ always speaks of God as of a father, that is, as if He were the condition of our existence."

August 2*nd*. Tolstoi and Marie Nikolaevna

were recalling a certain Voeikov. He was once a hussar, and then became a monk. When Tolstoi was young, Voeikov was continually at Yasnaya, permanently drunk, ragged, in monk's clothing, and telling lies unmercifully.

Tolstoi remembered a story that Voeikov told :

" ' We were once in a box : Mikhail Illariono-vich (Kutuzov), Alexander Pavlovich (Alexander I.), myself, and some one else. Sontag sang. She came out to the front of the stage. Her bosom—oh ! (he makes a gesture with his hand showing the size of her bust). Alexander Pavlovich said to me : " Voeikov, what is it ? " And I said to him : " An organism, Your Majesty ! " '

" And once, after all his mad ways and lies, he suddenly came up to me in the garden and said : ' I am tired of life, Levochka ! ' "

Marie Nikolaevna asked Tolstoi why he had never described Voeikov. Tolstoi said :

" There are some events and people in life, as there are scenes in nature, which cannot be described : they are too exceptional and seem to be impossible. Voeikov was like that. Dickens described such types."

August 3rd. The conversation turned on

Lobachevsky [1] and on his theory that space is of many dimensions. Tolstoi remembers Lobachevsky, who was Professor and Principal of the Kazan University when Tolstoi was an undergraduate there. Then the company began to recall various mathematicians, amongst whom there are often queer fellows to be met. Tolstoi mentioned Prince S. U. Urusov, the Sevastopol hero, who was a mathematician and a splendid chess player.

Tolstoi said of him :

" He used to get up at three o'clock in the morning, light his samovar, which was prepared for him the night before by his orderly, and begin his calculations. Urusov was trying to find a way of solving the different forms of equations. Later he went quite mad. Nothing came of his calculations. When, in the belief that he had arrived at a positive result, he decided to read a paper to the Mathematical Society, there was so awkward a silence after his paper was read that all felt ashamed." . . .

Tolstoi went on to say :

" I was always surprised that mathematicians who are so exact in their own science are so

---

[1] Nikolay Ivanovich Lobachevsky (1793–1856), the great Russian mathematician and geometrist (founder of the non - Euclidean geometry).

vague and inexact when they try to philosophize."

Tolstoi also mentioned Professors Nekrasov and B., whom he knew personally. Tolstoi recollected how one evening he visited B. :

" His wife was an unpleasant woman. That evening she was decolletée, and, as is always the case on such occasions, one feels something superfluous, unnecessary — one doesn't know where to look. Looking at her I remembered Turgenev's story, — how in Paris he always bought himself a loaf in the morning, and the baker's girl would hand it over to him with her bare arm, which was more like a leg than an arm."

August 20*th*. A certain gentleman from Petersburg (I don't remember his name) now and then sends books to Tolstoi. Recently he sent him the *Sovremennik* for 1852 in which Tolstoi's *Childhood* was published. Tolstoi read the books with great interest and said that the *Sovremennik* was at that time a very interesting review. Marie Nikolaevna, who was on a visit to Yasnaya, described how she read *Childhood* for the first time. She lived then with her husband in the country, in the Chernsky district of the Tula province, and Turgenev used to come to visit them fairly often. Her brother

Sergey Nikolaevich also lived there. During one visit Turgenev read them the MS. of his *Rudin*. Next time he brought a number of the *Sovremennik* and said to them:

" There is a wonderful new writer; a remarkable work by him is published here, *Childhood* "; and he began to read it aloud.

From the very first words Marie Nikolaevna and Sergey Nikolaevna were amazed:

" But he is describing us! Who is he? "

" At first we did not think of Levochka," Marie Nikolaevna went on. " He was in debt and had been sent to the Caucasus. We were rather inclined to think that our brother Nikolay had written *Childhood*."

It is said that Turgenev in his *Faust* described Marie Nikolaevna.

The conversation turned on Dostoevsky's hatred of Turgenev. Tolstoi greatly blamed the libel on Turgenev in *The Possessed*. This hatred always surprised Tolstoi, and so did that between Goncharov and Turgenev.

Tolstoi went on to say:

" Now books are written by people who have nothing to say. You read, but you do not see the writer. They always try to give ' the last word.' They reject the real writers and say that they have become obsolete. It is an absurd

Tolstoï said:

" When after the Sevastopol campaign I lived in Petersburg, Tyutchev, then a famous author, did me, a young writer, the honour to call on me. And then, I remember, how surprised I was that he, who had all his life mixed in court circles—he was a friend, in the purest sense, of the Empress Marie Alexandrovna—who spoke and wrote French more easily than Russian, picked out for special praise, when he expressed his admiration for my Sevastopol stories, a certain soldiers' expression; and this sensitiveness to the Russian language surprised me in him extraordinarily."

The conversation arose about writers' fees. Tolstoï turned to P. Biryukov and said:

" I understand fees in the case of a work like your biography (of Tolstoï), but fees to writers for their artistic work always seemed strange and wrong to me. The man wrote and enjoyed writing, and suddenly for that enjoyment he asks five hundred roubles per printed sheet!" . . .

Tolstoï said:

" I became more and more convinced that a sensible man is to be known by his humility. Conceit is incompatible with understanding."

notion—to become obsolete. Modern books are read just because one can get to know ' the last word' from them; and this is easier than to read and know the real writers. These purveyors of ' the last word' do enormous harm, they make people unused to thinking independently."

Some one mentioned Kant, and Tolstoï said:

" What is particularly valuable in Kant is that he always thought for himself. In reading him you deal all the time with *his* thoughts, and this is extraordinarily valuable."

About reading modern literature Tolstoï said:

" I am much more ready to read the memoirs of some old General in the *Russkaia Starina*; he romances a little, like Zavalishin, about his merits and successes, but this can be excused, and there is always something of interest in it."

Tolstoï said further:

" Brain work often tires the head, and when tired, you can't work as fruitfully as with a fresh head. Generally speaking, in brain work the moment is very important. There are moments when your thoughts come out as if moulded in bronze; at other moments nothing happens."

December 31*st*. Tolstoï said:

" I am always interested to see what can become obsolete in literature. I am curious to know what in modern literature will seem old-fashioned, as, for instance, Karamzin's 'Oh soever!' etc., seems to us now. Within my memory it has become impossible to write a long poem in verse. It seems to me that in time works of art will cease to be invented. It will be a shame to invent a story about a fictitious Ivan Ivanovich or Marie Petrovna. Writers, if such there be, will not invent, but will only describe the significant or interesting things which they have happened to observe in life."

1906

August 21*st*. Speaking abou
said :
    " Great works of art are for all
exist. They must only be revealed
Angelo said."
    Tolstoi was reminded by this
Michael Angelo's of a peasant who w
training cut wonderful figures in w
said, when Tolstoi expressed surprise a
with which he did it :
    " It is inside there. I am only tak
what is not needed."

    Tolstoi said that Turgenev, in his e
over Pushkin's description of Lensky's dea
Onegin, said that the wonderful rhyme—*r*
stranen—seemed to be inevitable.
    Then Tolstoi recollected certain of Tyutche
poems, whom he rates very highly.
    I asked him if he knew Tyutchev.

Of conceit Tolstoi said a long time ago in my presence :

" Every man can be seen as a fraction, whose numerator is his actual qualities, and its denominator his opinion of himself. The greater the denominator the less is the absolute quantity of the fraction."

1907

September 7th. Tolstoi went to-day to Mme.
Zveginzev to ask the police inspector, who lives
on her estate, to release from prison the house-
painter, Ivan Grigorevich ; and also to thank
her for the peaches she had sent him.

Tolstoi said :

" There was her daughter, Princess Volkonsky,
there. They all wanted to direct me on the
path of truth. I tried to speak with all serious-
ness ; but hardly anything could penetrate
through their diamonds and luxury. They now
employ the stove-maker who used to come to
me to borrow books. And he has been telling
them that I said that one should not believe in
God, and various other bits of nonsense. I told
them that there was nothing strange in my words
being distorted. If even from Christ's teaching
people can deduce the rites of the Church, the
blessing of war, etc., then it is no wonder that our
words are always misrepresented and distorted.

" Then they asked me how I explained the fact that in my family no one followed my teaching. I told them that it probably happened because I lived like a Pharisee, and did not fulfil my own teaching. To this they made no reply."

Tolstoi said that he saw to-day a review of a new book on Turgenev. The book is partly of a polemical kind. The author gives an account of Turgenev's quarrels with all writers (Dostoevsky, Tolstoi, Hertzen, Fet, etc.), as if it were his object to vindicate Turgenev and to prove that on all occasions he was right.

Tolstoi said :

" Really, it is strange that he quarrelled with every one. He was a very nice, good man. Only he was very weak, and was conscious of his weakness. Once, I remember, Count Urusov was here, my good friend. There were two brothers, and for some reason people considered them stupid. Now knowing this, Turgenev began arguing with them arrogantly as though feeling his superiority, but Urusov quietly, easily, and confidently refuted his argument. And no wonder : Urusov had his own definite religious convictions, whatever they might be, and Turgenev had none."

" I was fond of him," Tolstoi said of Turgenev.

Sophie Andreevna said that Turgenev had loved Tolstoi very much.

"No, on the contrary," Tolstoi replied. "He rather liked me as a writer, but, as man, I did not find in him real warmth and cordiality. Well, he liked no one in that way, except women with whom he happened to be in love. He had no friends."

Tolstoi asked me about my work, whether I was composing music, and said how bad it was when people force work out of themselves, and how great artists lose by immediately starting a new work when they have finished the old one.

Tolstoi mentioned Pushkin and said :

"The best writers are always strict with themselves. I re-write until I feel that I am beginning to spoil. And then, of course, I leave it alone. And one begins to spoil because at first, when you enjoy your work, whilst it is *yours*, you apply all your spiritual force to it. Later when the fundamental original idea ceases more and more to be new, and becomes, as it were, someone else's, it bores you. You begin to try to say something new and you spoil and distort the first idea."

A telegram arrived from Leonid Andreev asking to be allowed to come.

Tolstoi said :

" How terribly undeserved fame, like that of Andreev, spoils a man ! "

Then Tolstoi could not compose a telegram in reply.

" How shall I answer ? ' Come.' . . . But that is too short. ' Shall be very glad to see you ' —that is not altogether true. Well, Dushan Petrovich, write simply : ' You are welcome.' "

Tolstoi said :

" I had a letter to-day from a man who congratulates me on my fifty-fifth anniversary, and writes that he so much loves my works that he is always reading and re-reading *War and Peace*, for instance, but he says : ' However much I tried, I could not read a single one of your philosophical writings to the end.' He tries to persuade me to give up that kind of writing."

" Why should he have written all that ? " Tolstoi said, laughing. " There was a man living and nobody knew he was a fool, and suddenly he got up and told me so ! " . . .

1908

January 6th. Yesterday, when many letters came, Tolstoi said :

" In old age one becomes indifferent to the fact that one will never see the results of one's activity. But the results will be there. It is not modesty on my part, but I know there will be results."

To - day, speaking of the revolutionaries, Tolstoi said :

" Their chief mistake is the superstition that one can arrange human life."

April 12th. Tatyana Lvovna was saying that A. N. Volkov is writing a book on art. Tolstoi became interested. Volkov says in his book that art must follow Nature blindly in everything.

Tolstoi said :

" It is absolutely untrue. It is always like that. When people are discussing art, they either say, like the modern decadents, that everything is allowed, everything is possible, that there is complete freedom in art. Or they talk about the slavish imitation of Nature. Both views are false. Just as every man is perfectly individual and never occurs twice over, so also his thoughts, his feelings are always new ; they are *his* thoughts and feelings alone. At the basis of a true work of art there must lie some perfectly original idea or feeling, but it must be expressed with slavish adherence to the smallest details of life."

July 27th. A fortnight ago Mme. E—v, the wife of a privy councillor, came here on a visit. Tolstoi played chess with me on the balcony and the lady talked at first to Sophie Andreevna, and then, I think, to Marie Nikolaevna, about the great service which landowners performed, and how the peasants are beasts, and how, but for the landed aristocracy and their culture, they would become absolute brutes.

Tolstoi kept silent, but at last could stand it no longer. He got up from his chair and said to her :

"You must forgive me, but what you are saying is terrible, one can't listen to it with indifference. If one is speaking of beasts, then certainly it is not the peasants who are beasts,

but all of us who rob them and live on them.
And all the 'work' of the landowners is nothing
but playing about for want of anything else to
do ! "

Tolstoi was in a state of agitation and could
not get calm for a long time afterwards.

The same evening at tea, when Mme. E—v
had gone, the talk was about executions. Sophie
Andreevna tried to prove that any murder is as
bad as an execution, and yet people don't talk
about them. Elisabetha Valerianovna replied
that an execution is a murder which is considered to be just, and the horror of it lies in that.

Tolstoi said :

" If one were to ask who is worse, the
wretched executioner, hired, intoxicated, spiritu-
ally destroyed, or those who hire him and those
who pass sentence of death, the prosecutors, the
judges, then it seems to me there can be no
doubt."

At tea Elisabetha Valerianovna asked her
mother, Marie Nikolaevna, to have some milk,
and she began to drink it.

Tolstoi said :

" How is it, Mashenka, that you drink it?
For myself, if I am told to drink milk, I want
sherry, and, when I'm told to drink sherry, I
want milk." . . .

Marie Nikolaevna began recalling the past. When they lived in Moscow, soon after the death of their father in 1837–38, Tolstoi, who was then about eight or nine, jumped out of the first-floor window and was badly hurt.

Tolstoi said :

" I remember that quite well. I wanted to see what would happen, and I even remember that, as I jumped, I tried to jump upwards."

July 28th. Yesterday my wife and I were at Yasnaya. Tolstoi's leg is still painful. He lies in a chair with it stretched out. He suffers from inflammation and from embolism of the vein. They say he must lie like that for six weeks.

We arrived at Yasnaya about eight o'clock. Tolstoi sat in a chair in the dining-room. He played chess with S. Then he began to play chess with me. S. looked on at our game for a time, and then sitting near the round table he began to talk to Sophie Andreevna about the children's anthology to be chosen from Tolstoi's works, which he wishes to publish for his Jubilee (Tolstoi's eighty years). The conversation was terrible. Sophie Andreevna said in the sharpest way that she was not going to be cheated out of her rights, that she would go to a lawyer and would write to the papers about it.

S. behaved rather well, and asked her to point out what she would allow to be published ; but she would not listen to reason. At last she said that it was the same as if he stole her silver spoons. It was intolerably humiliating and painful.

Sophie Andreevna made attempts to draw Tolstoi into the dispute. Poor Tolstoi ! He suffered, frowned, shook his head in horror, but kept silent. The greatest deed in his life is his humility and patience with Sophie Andreevna. His behaviour is all the more difficult, because people criticize him for being humble and long-suffering in this way. How much easier it would be for him to leave this kind of life, which he not only does not want, but which is intolerable to him.

Then it became even worse. S. left the room for a time, and when he returned and sat down near us watching the chess, Sophie Andreevna did not see him and began talking about something and, as usual, complaining of the worries of managing the household, and said :

" When I get rid of the steward, of the thieving, of S., and . . ." of something else, I don't remember what.

Every one was overcome with shame. Tolstoi even uttered a groan. S. turned deadly white.

Some one managed to whisper to Sophie Andreevna that he, S., was in the room. She was not in the least put out, and only began saying how much she regretted that she had not died under her operation.

Tolstoi glanced at S.; S. said:

" Did you want to say something, Leo Nikolaevich ? "

Tolstoi was silent for a time and then said :

" You understood me."

Then he added :

" Whom God loves, him He tries."

It was intolerable. S. left the room quickly and went away without saying good-bye to any one.

There the matter rested. Mme. Zveginzev then arrived. Tolstoi talked about Chertkov's father : [1]

" When he was about forty-five, gangrene attacked his toe. Then it went further, and his leg had to be amputated at the knee. He went to England. There they made him an artificial leg on which he walked fairly easily. Then the gangrene attacked the other leg. This, too, had to be amputated, but this time much above the knee. He sat in a chair and was carried about. He was very patient and did not groan, although

[1] Gregory Ivanovich Chertkov (1828–1884), Adjutant-General.

he shuddered with pain all day long. In the evenings he would be given an injection of morphia; he would then revive, read the papers, and talk. He was a brilliant man, a wit, and a great success in society. He used to be taken in his chair to parties. There was even a cult for him; he used to visit the Empress. In society invitations were issued: 'Venez; M. Chertkoff sera ce soir chez nous.' He died early. He never drank and never could drink, for the wine went to his head. But once at dinner some one drank, and he took a little glass of vodka, and suddenly died then and there at the dinner party."

Some one began to talk about bugs.

Tolstoi said:

"When he has bugs, Perna does not scratch, but lies quietly—he allows them to have their fill, like Buddha, who gave himself to be devoured by the tigress; and when the bugs have eaten enough, he sleeps peacefully. In olden days, under the serfdom, when the landed gentry lived very dirtily and bugs were everywhere, if a guest remained for the night, the butler used to be put into the bed first, so as to feed the bugs, and only after that was the bed made for the guest."

Then I came up to Tolstoi and he talked to

me.   At first, with a smile, he winked at Mme. Zveginzev's colossal hat.

I asked him if he was still working on the new " Circle of Reading."   Tolstoi said that he is already working at the twenty-first day.   He makes the same number of days in all the twelve months.   I told him that I had read the first day and that it seemed to me very good.

Tolstoi said :

" Yes, but it must all be gone over again. At the beginning of each day I put the ideas which can be understood by children and simple people.   This is very difficult.   I am doing it now, when I am an old man, but I ought to have begun my career as a writer by doing it.   I ought to have written so that it could be understood by every one.   This is true, too, of your art. And, generally speaking, of all the arts."

I said to him that in music the most musical language happens to be beyond one's reach, whether or not one belongs to intellectual circles, either because one is not trained or because one is unmusical by nature.

Tolstoi agreed with me partly, but said that this was the case in other arts as well :

" There are some ideas which can be understood by all and are necessary to all, but are expressed in the language of a small group of people. For instance, the poem ' I remember the wonderful moment,' or ' When to the mortal the noisy day passes into silence '—do you remember them ? A peasant couldn't understand them."

Tolstoi said :

" I was thinking a great deal about art to-day and I re-read my article, and I must confess I agreed with my ideas."

Tolstoi is reading the English biography of Chopin (by Huneker). He does not like it. He said to me :

" I have not read books of that kind for a long time. The author does not reveal Chopin's inner life, but displays his own erudition, his ability to write well and wittily. He is controversial and proves the faults of other biographers. But there is no Chopin here. . . . Yet there are many interesting facts in it. It is the life of a small circle of poets, writers, and musicians—what a perverted and terrible life ! And George Sand, that disgusting woman ! . . . I can't understand her success."

Marie Nikolaevna, who was listening, said :

" No ! she has done good things. Take, for instance, her *Consuelo*."

" No, that is not good. It is all false and bad and tedious ; I could never read it."

July 30*th*. There were staying at Yasnaya Marie Alexandrovna, I. Gorbunov, and E. I. Popov. Tolstoi was not well. His leg was still painful. We played chess. Then there was tea. Before the game of chess, when I had come into the drawing-room by myself, Tolstoi was telling Obolensky and the others, whom I mentioned, the plot of Anatole France's novel, a very complicated novel. I believe it is called *Jocaste*. Tolstoi was telling the plot in detail and was surprised at its absurdity, but said it was written with A. France's usual mastery.

As I came in, I had met two men downstairs who wished to see Tolstoi. As Tolstoi is ill, Gusev (the secretary) went downstairs. One of the men turned out to be a sectarian, " an immortalist," and the other sent up by Gusev a strange note in which, referring to Boulanger's promise to try to find a job for him, he said something foolish about his desire to be useful to Tolstoi. Altogether there was no sense, no purpose in it.

Tolstoi said:

" It is amazing, why can't they understand? It seems to him that only he and myself exist, and yet there are hundreds of him, and only one of me. And what can I do for him? "

At tea Tolstoi talked about the 'immortalist.'
Marie Nikolaevna asked what sect it was.

Tolstoi said to her :

" The 'immortalists' believe that if they go
on believing they will never die. And when
one of them dies they say : he did not really
believe. . . . I quite understand it. With them
immortality is identified with the body. At a
low level of religious development that is understandable. The Church doctrine also thinks of
resurrection as a resurrection in the flesh."

Marie Nikolaevna began to say that she
believed that there *would* be something after
death.

Tolstoi said :

" In the first place, as to our state after death,
it is impossible to say that it *will* be. Immortality neither will be, nor was, but *is*. It is
outside the forms of time and space. People
who keep on asking what is going to happen
after death should be told : the very same thing
that *was* before birth. We do not know, neither
can we or must we know what existence outside
of the body, fusion with God, is like, and, when
people begin telling me about it—even if some
one from the other world were to come to tell
me about it—I would not believe and I should
say that I do not need it. That which we need,

we always are aware of and know without doubting. One ought to live so that one's life should help on the happiness of other people."

Marie Nikolaevna said that although she neither believes in nor admits the existence of paradise and hell with real suffering, nevertheless there is hell for the soul in the constant suffering which comes from realization of evil done or of good undone.

" I can't admit," she added, " that one who lives badly and has done no good will achieve the same fusion with God as the man who has lived justly."

Tolstoi was about to say something, but Marie Nikolaevna interrupted him.

Tolstoi said quietly and gently :

" I listened to you, Mashenka ; now do you listen to me. Compared with the perfection of God, the difference which exists in life between the most righteous man and the most wicked is so insignificant that it is simply equal to nothing. And how am I to admit that God, the God whom I realize through love, can be revengeful and punish ? "

" But suppose one lived wickedly all one's life and died without repenting ? " Marie Niko-laevna said.

" Ah, Mashenka," Tolstoi said, " but what

man wishes to be bad? The man whom we think bad we must love and pity for his sufferings. Nobody wants to live a bad life and to suffer. He must not be punished, he must be pitied, because he does not know the truth."

Marie Nikolaevna still could not give up her point of view.

Tolstoi said to her:

"Very well, if what you believe in satisfies you; and this must never be condemned, only you must not prevent people from believing what their conscience prompts them to, and you must not try to make them believe differently, as all the Churches do, the Catholic, the Protestant, the Orthodox, the Buddhist, the Muhammadan."

. . .

Towards the end of July, Klechkovsky came to Yasnaya and played.

Tolstoi lay on the sofa, and, after Klechkovsky had finished playing, we sat by Tolstoi. Klechkovsky began talking about himself, how dissatisfied he was with his life, how he would like to live on the land, to give up his music teaching and the Institute. But he can't do it because his father would be much upset by such a sudden change in his life. He also said that he would like to go and live in a community.

Tolstoi replied to him:

" Why in a community? One ought not to separate oneself from other people. If there is anything good in a man, let that light be spread about him wherever he lives. What numbers of people settled in communities, yet nothing came of it ! All their energies went at first into external arrangement of life, and when at length they settled down, there began to be quarrels and gossip, and it all fell to pieces. . . . You are grumbling at the Institute, yet there is the porter there whom you could treat kindly, like a human being, and then you would have done a good act. And the girls, your pupils ? Can't you make a great deal that is good out of those relations ? One can always shut oneself off from people, but nothing good will come of it. I say this not because I want to justify my own life. I live in the wrong way and know it is the wrong way, but I have always wanted and tried to live better, only I could not. . . . I shall go to God in the consciousness that I did what I could to make my life better.

" One should never attempt to arrange life beforehand. At times I ask myself what I should do if I remained here alone ? For instance, I should say to Ilya Vasilevich : ' It would be nice if you did the rooms and tidied them to-day, and I will do them to-morrow.'

197

Then we should eat together. And so on with one thing after another, as things would arrange themselves. Only it has to be remembered that the ideal of the material life cannot be fully realized, any more than the ideal of the spiritual life. The whole point is in the constant effort to approach the ideal. If I gave up everything now and went away, Sophie Andreevna would hate me, and the evil of that would perhaps be worse. You have your father . . . and so it is with every one."

Tolstoi said before this :

" I said to Sophie Andreevna to-day, and I believe she was hurt by it : the first concern in life must be for the things of the soul, and, if household duties interfere with that, then damn household duties."

Last night we sat on the balcony.

Tolstoi said that he had had a nice letter from a simple man who had read several of his books, and who asked, at the end of his letter, where there were people who live a Christian life, for he would leave everything and go and live with them. Tolstoi said that he replied to him much in the same way as he had done to Klechkovsky.

Tolstoi added :

" I think that even if one was a woman in a

brothel, or a gaoler, one ought not suddenly to give up one's work. Certainly any one who realizes the evil of such a life will not go on with it, but the important thing is not the external change."

Tolstoi said he had received three letters : one from Mr. Grekov, who sent him three copies of his book, *The Message of Peace*, and wrote that his book was so remarkable that, if it were widely read, it would revolutionize human life ; the second letter was from an intellectual who asked for a loan of 800 roubles ; and the third from a simple illiterate peasant, a good serious letter. Tolstoi said that, besides letters asking for money, he also receives letters from authors sending him their books, and begging that Tolstoi will use his authority to make their books known.

" An odd idea," Tolstoi said, " that I should try to spread opinions which I neither sympathize with nor share."

August 5th. Marie Nikolaevna told how the steward Fokanich had once stolen 400 roubles from Tolstoi, and Tolstoi took it rather indifferently. Soon afterwards Sergey Nikolaevich, Tolstoi's brother, was very much worried about his affairs, and when he was told that it was not worth while to be so worried, he said :

" It doesn't matter to Levochka that Fokanich stole 400 roubles from him ; he will write a story and get the money back ; and he will describe Fokanich into the bargain ; but where shall I get my money ? "

Tolstoi replied to this :

" Mashenka, how can you remember all this ? But I heard an expression to-day that keeps on coming back into my mind."

And Tolstoi told how during lunch to-day an unusually importunate beggar arrived. He stood by the balcony and began saying how happy he was to see and salute Tolstoi, etc. . . . He was given something, but he was not satisfied, went to the kitchen, and began begging with extraordinary importunity. After lunch when Tolstoi was coming down from the balcony, Ilya Vasilevich, pointing to the beggar, said to Tolstoi :

" Yes, that fellow could beg the parson's mare off him."

August 19*th*. At tea the conversation turned upon modern literature. Tolstoi asked Buturlin to send him anything new he could find by Anatole France, whom Tolstoi values very highly. He spoke again.

Tolstoi said :

"I cannot remember getting a strong impression from a book for a long time. I do not think it is because I am old; it seems to me that modern literature, like the Roman literature in the past, is coming to an end. There is no one, neither in the West nor here."

Buturlin asked Tolstoi if he remembered Oscar Wilde's *De Profundis*.

Tolstoi had not read it, but said:

"I forget everything now, but I remember having tried to read Wilde, and it has left me with an impression that he was not worth reading."

Speaking of modern Russian writers Tolstoi mentioned Kuprin.

"His scope is small; he knows the life of the soldiers, but still he has real artistic power. The others simply have nothing to say, and are on the look-out for new forms. But why look for new forms? If you have something to say, you should only ask for time in which to say what you want, but you won't need to seek new forms."

Apropos of Eltzbacher's book on anarchy, which Tolstoi was re-reading, he said:

"Christian anarchy is a narrow definition of the Christian conception of the world, but anarchy follows certainly from Christianity in its application to social life."

September 3rd. Tolstoi again spoke about the old German mystic, Angelus Silesius. Tolstoi asked some one to fetch his book (a large old volume) and read aloud several aphorisms, translating them as he read. When he came to the passage: " If God did not love Himself in us, we could neither love ourselves, nor God," Tolstoi exclaimed :

" Ah, how well that's said ! "

Referring to some account in the papers of a conversation with him, Tolstoi said :

" If I were to live for another eighty years, and were never to cease talking, I could not manage to say all the sayings that are attributed to me."

September 6th. Tolstoi said, with reference to the addresses and congratulations on his eightieth birthday (August 28th, 1908) which keep on coming :

" I believe I am right in saying that I have no vanity, but I can't help being touched involuntarily. And yet, at my age, I live so far away from all this, it is all so unnecessary and so humiliating. Only one thing is necessary, the inner life of the spirit."

On August 29th, when more than two thousand telegrams of congratulation arrived, Tolstoi said :

" I feel with joy that I have utterly lost the power of being interested in all this. In the past, I remember, I experienced a feeling of pride ; I was glad at my success. But now— and I think it is not false modesty—it is a matter of absolute indifference to me. Perhaps it is because I have had too much success. It is like sweets : if you have too many, you feel surfeited. But one thing is pleasant : in nearly all the letters, congratulations, addresses, the same thing is repeated—it has simply become a truism —that I have destroyed religious delusions and opened the way for the search after truth. If it is true, it is just what I have wanted and tried to do all my life, and this is very dear to me."

1909

February 10*th*. Once in the winter Sophie
Andreevna in Tolstoi's presence criticized V. G.
Chertkov bitterly, which, as usual, pained him
very much. This was in the morning. In the
middle of the conversation Tolstoi got up and
went into his room.

Some time later he came into the dining-
room, stood at the door, and said in an agitated
voice :

" There is an old nurse in our house. I
scarcely know her, but I love her because she
loves Sasha, and when there is nothing like that
in a house, there is no real love." . . .

After saying this, Tolstoi turned and quietly
went to his room.

To-night Tolstoi said :

" When one listens to music, it agitates,
excites, elates, but one does not think. But when
I play patience in my room, the finest thoughts
come to me."

During work, especially if he found some difficulty, Tolstoi used to play patience. This was his habit throughout his life. When he was writing Part III. of *Resurrection*, Tolstoi was undecided for a long time about the fate of Katyusha Maslov. Now he decided that Nekhlyudov should marry her, now that he should not. At last he decided to play a game of patience : if the patience came out, Nekhlyudov should marry her; if not, then he should not marry her. The patience did not come out. Once Tolstoi told me that he had found a passage in a book, which he was writing, very difficult. He hesitated for a long time what to do, but made up his mind and wrote it. Then he decided to test it by means of a game of patience; if the patience came out, that meant that what he had written was good; if it did not come out, then it was bad. The patience did not come out, and Tolstoi said to himself: "Never mind, it is good as it is!" and he left it as he had written it.

May 24th. Tolstoi was speaking about Dietrich's German book on Goethe. The author sent him the book and asked him his opinion.
Tolstoi said :
"It is amazing ! So far back as 1824 Goethe

wrote that sincerity was become almost impossible in art, because of the multitude of newspapers, journals, and reviews. The artist reads them, involuntarily pays attention to them, and cannot be perfectly sincere. What would he say if he lived now! "

THE END